SHOOT THIS ONE

GRANT.

ESSAYS BY
JAVIER GRILLO-MARXUACH

"Shoot This One"
Essays by Javier Grillo-Marxuach

This version first published in paperback in 2015 by
Puppet Bureau.

Copyright © 2015 Javier Grillo-Marxuach

ISBN: 978-1507754672

Cover design and Typesetting by Lee Thompson
Cover illustrations by Grant Carmichael

Printed and bound by CreateSpace

Puppet Bureau
www.puppetbureau.com

SHOOT THIS ONE

ESSAYS BY
JAVIER GRILLO-MARXUACH

CONTENTS

INTRODUCTION

by Maureen Ryan

I once went out to dinner with three TV writer/ producers, and we got very drunk. Perhaps our collective level of inebriation is germane, perhaps not. What I can say for sure is that I look back on that night with great fondness, not just because the Italian food was delicious and the red wine never stopped flowing.

I have such affection for that evening in large part because of the stories that were told. One set of interlocking sagas was particularly memorable: The most senior of the three writer/ producers I dined with -- I'll call him Writer A -- regaled us with tales of the behavior of a legendary star with whom he'd worked on an ill-fated project.

If I told you the names of the shows Writer A has worked or revealed the name of the Big Star who headlined this Television Hindenburg, trust me, you'd be as agog as I was that night. Nothing is juicier and more delicious than gossip delivered by someone whose primary skill set revolves around telling stories. If someone can tell a tale well on screen, chances are his or her conversation is damn near transfixing after the third bottle of Sangiovese.

At this point, I'll stipulate that Javier Grillo-Marxuach was not one of the TV writers around that table. I'm fairly sure he has gotten drunk on wine at some point (how one can work in television and not do so nightly is a mystery to me). And, thanks to this book, I know that he's worked with monsters (both the talented and the untalented kinds). Still, he wasn't the guy unspooling the "All the

Things That Went So Terribly Wrong" tale that night. But trust me, this frustratingly vague recounting of one drunken dinner in Los Angeles does have a connection to his book.

It's not just because both Writer A and Javi believe strongly in the need to interrogate failure in order to learn from it. It's not just because both have been in the entertainment industry long enough to see the best and the worst that artistic collaborators are capable of. It's because that dinner and this book have a lot in common (though your purchase of Javi's volume does not get you any lasagna -- sorry).

What I remember most about the Night of Too Much Wine is that it demonstrated just how much Writer A loved the medium of television. Wait, what? He spent an hour or two telling his dining companions about how good intentions and respectful meetings had descended into a hellscape of slammed doors, tense conversations and volcanic anger. (It was funnier the way he told it.)

How did I get up from that meal and, through a woozy haze, realize that this battle-scared veteran cared even more about TV more than I'd thought? It was because, like all truly memorable stories, the Television Hindenburg tale contained a few valuable lessons. Sure, we all enjoyed hearing about the unbridled gall of an American Legend, who, as it turned out, was capable of behaving like an American Nightmare.

But that wasn't the lesson, because over the course of more than 100 years of media coverage of Hollywood, the idea might have bubbled up, just once or twice, that people who are rich and famous can be assholes.

(Sidebar: In my experience, that kind of behavior is very much the exception to the rule. Perhaps it's because the people in the industry behave when dealing with the media because they have such great respect for us. [Let's pause for a moment while I wait for you to stop laughing.] Really, I wish I had a font of stories about industry people behaving like total jerkweeds, but the vast majority of folks I've come across have been hard-working, well-intentioned, and reasonable, and even if we have disagreed about something, the industry folk -- actors, writers, executives, whatever -- have generally managed to be civil when doing so.)

(Except for That One Asshole, but perhaps that story will serve as the preface to *my* book.)

Anyway, the lessons were embedded in the fact that Writer A had stood up to the Star and fought bad choices that were being made for the project. He said the one word you're not supposed to say unequivocally in Hollywood: No.

(Sidebar 2: You could easily come up with a list of 100 ways that entertainment-industry people say no without saying the word "no," i.e., "She didn't respond to the material," which, in regular-person speak, means: "Good God, that script is a pile of steaming horseshit." Seriously, there are so many other ways that people say no; I collect them like other people collect Hummels. But I get understand this tendency to minimize and placate; outside of ant colonies or Wall Street, few places in the world are as hierarchical and interconnected as the entertainment industry, and few individuals have the kind of pull that allows them to say "no" bluntly or rudely without having to care about the consequences.)

In the course of the Television Hindenburg donnybrook, Writer A was diplomatic and professional at all times, but eventually, he drew a line in the sand and wound up winning some of the creative battles he'd been fighting. The project ultimately went down in flames, but that didn't mean he loved his profession any less -- in fact, he proved by his actions that he really *did* love his work.

He fought for the project, you see. Not for his ego, not for his salary, not for his prestige, not to salvage his connections and potential working relationships. Saying no and not giving in is hard to do for anyone, but a TV writer can't say he or she really loves telling stories on screen -- not really -- unless that writer willing to do that when it counts.

Writer A would do it again, and I've known many other men and women in the industry who've done just that -- drawn lines, said no, fought bad ideas, put their asses on the line. Of course, it's an industry built on compromise, and as many stories in Javi's book demonstrate, any writer who thinks she or he can ignore the collaborative nature of the TV industry is in for a painful ride. TV is not the industry to choose if you absolutely *must* be the True Rebel, the lone wolf whose singular vision must triumph at every turn. If that's going to be your pose, good luck with that.

That said, those who've lasted, those whose shows I've written about and thought about and cared about -- those people are willing to stand up for something that seems fanciful, chimerical: an idea, a story, an image, a character.

You might say, "Isn't it unwise for someone to put their sanity and livelihood on the line for things that don't actually exist?"

To which I say, p'shaw. Of course they exist. Haven't you read *Harry Potter*?

I'm not saying Hogwarts really exists (though there's

a damn fine replica of it in Orlando. I'm actually serious. I love the theme park known as "*The Wizarding World of Harry Potter,*" and I'm not ashamed to say it.) But I do love stories about wizards and incantations and spells and magic and fantastical worlds full of people and creatures whose emotional dilemmas seem absolutely real. Give me a quest and a wizard, and I'm a happy camper.

"But those kinds of books are just works of escapism," you say. Nope. Most of them are not. The best ones evoke deeply relatable emotions. But there's another reason I love those books: Because words *do* change the world.

Think about the vows that people say on the day they get married. If you bio-scanned the vow-sayers the day before the ceremony and the day after, those scans would likely look identical (allowing for cake and champagne consumption, of course).

But those two people would *feel* different. Because of words that were said -- and documents that were signed. Is it the pieces of paper that makes the difference? To some degree, but I can cite other examples of spells that work real, palpable magic. Think about the time that someone important in your life said "I love you" to you for the first time.

Didn't those words have meaning? Didn't they change things? Don't words like that weave a spell of their own?

The life of a TV writer is one of takeout food, deadlines, rumpled clothing, and insecurity. As you can tell from these essays, there are many ways to fail and succeed, and having an open mind, good intentions, a devotion to craft and a great work ethic guarantees a TV writer exactly nothing. So why does anyone stick with it?

Because a few days after a TV writer turns in a script,

those words become reality. Those words are said by actors, and if that writer is lucky, the audience will be moved. Viewers will argue about that episode, they'll praise it, they'll create gifs, they'll cosplay at conventions, and sometimes they'll rage at those idiots on the writing staff who have no idea what they're doing. Within one season of television, fans and critics may engage in all of the above and more.

Whatever the feedback, writers often stick with this particular career because, deep down, they know their words can create magic; they can change the world. American television has a long way to go before it truly reflects the diversity of America, but, day after day, week after week, decade after decade, many different kinds of shows have made us think harder about racism, sexism, class, morality, gender and ethics. (Preferably while aliens were blowing things up, of course.) TV doesn't let us be, it probes and pokes at things and uses words and pictures to make us think, feel, question. Skilled writers, whatever their medium, take us deeper into the unending labyrinth inside us all, and if a book or TV show or movie has ever made you cry, then you know I'm right: Words aren't just words, they're magic.

Unlike a writer of fantasy fiction or wizardly tales, however, Javi is willing to open up the hood and tell you exactly how it's done. I'm fairly sure that if it is your ambition to be a writer -- or any kind of storyteller, really -- reading this book will not just entertain you but spare you some heartache and headaches as you embark on this magical, heartbreaking, brain-melting path. But if you have no ambitions as a writer and you're just a consumer of entertainment or a citizen of the world, you will likely find food for thought in these pages.

What Javi does in these essays is combine the insight of a good coroner, the diagnostic abilities of an experienced mechanic, and the enthusiasm of a passionate inventor (and that is, I just realized, a pretty good pitch for a TV show: if anyone is interested in "Captain Cadaver's Adventure Garage," call my agent).

I've been lucky enough to spend much of the past 15 years talking to writers, producers and actors about the creative choices they've made and the stories they've told. But as is only right and proper, those of us in the media generally tell those stories as outsiders. I don't live in Los Angeles, and drunken dinners with TV producers are not a regular fixture of my life (I actually don't drink very often, as it happens). Some of the usefulness of critics derives from the fact that we are outside Hollywood kitchen, as it were. We just tell you if the meal is any good.

But Javi's background as a writer, an executive, and a producer give him a very different and most illuminating perspective on the many revolutions that have overtaken TV in the last couple of decades. And like the kind of dogged forensic investigator you see all over TV these days, Javi takes apart all kinds of things and digs into their guts. Death, politics, self-hatred, curiosity, joy, despair and what it means to truly learn and what one gains by losing -- all of these topics go under his gentle but firm scalpel. The older I get, the more I think that the two most important qualities anyone can possess are curiosity and compassion. Whether you agree or disagree with Javi's conclusions, I think you'll find every essay displays both, plus a gentle wit and brisk pacing.

Speaking of pacing, I should wrap this up. Let's return to the night I went out with those TV writers. Silly me, I brought along an audio recorder that evening. Given that

Writer A had been in the business for much longer than the two other scribes, I thought I'd get some kind of "Veteran Shares Insights With Up-And-Comers" piece out of our conversation. But as the dinner progressed, the stories went way off the record, and Writer A asked that I avoid the Television Hindenburg tale, because he might recount it himself in book or essay form one day.

Every so often, he'd look over at the tape recorder and say, "You can't use that." Eventually, I realized that none of the conversation was going to be usable, and I turned the recorder off. I did gain insights into those writers' careers and into certain aspects of the industry, but what transpired around the table would not be anything I'd be able to easily boil down into an 800-word story.

But that's one of my main memories of that night: Writer A glancing over at the metal rectangle of my recorder and saying, "You can't use that," as he unspooled tales of enthusiasm and despair, silliness and integrity, creativity, and folly.

Javi's book contains more of the same, but there's a key difference: You *can* use this.

Maureen Ryan
January 2015

Maureen Ryan is the television critic for *The Huffington Post*. Before that, she was the television critic for *The Chicago Tribune*. Before that, she still watched too much TV.

GILDING THE SMALL SCREEN: OR, "IS IT JUST ME OR DID TV GET GOOD ALL OF A SUDDEN?"

This much-expanded version of a lecture I delivered at the University of Michigan, Department of Screen Arts and Cultures on November 12, 2012, was published online by the Los Angeles Review of Books *on September 24th, 2014.*

People whose job it is to declare the comings and goings of Golden Ages of things agree that the "Golden Age of Television" began in the mid-1950s. That's when the medium, only milliseconds past its infancy, simultaneously delivered a near-catastrophic blow to the feature film industry and became a cigarette smoke-filled bullpen where the great middlebrow drama of the Chayefskys, Footes, and Serlings mingled with the live comedy of the Caesars and Berles while the Sevareids and Murrows rolled up their shirt sleeves and fought demagoguery from the corner office.

More recently, the explosion of "quality television" in the wake of the 1998 and 1999 premieres of *Sex and the City* and *The Sopranos* has led many (especially those who profit from TV) to declare that a new Golden Age is upon us. This "Second Golden Age" has stolen the mantle of the auteur cinema of the late 1960s and '70s and the independent films of the '90s as the pinnacle of thoughtful, character- and theme-driven entertainment for the mass audience.

While I feel about Golden Ages the way Groucho Marx felt about clubs that would have him as a member, I suppose it would be fair to say that -- as one of the Emmy Award-winning writer/producers of *Lost* (a Second Golden Age stalwart that celebrates the 10th anniversary of its premiere this week) -- I have had a ringside seat for whatever it is you call the current wave of pop culture. From that vantage point, I feel that I can provide some perspective on the hows and whys for the sudden explosion of creative ambition in a medium which -- for decades prior -- was mostly the prefix to the suffix "is a vast wasteland."

When *Lost* was called onstage to receive the Best Dramatic Series Emmy in 2005, I was the chubby guy in the Nehru jacket and thick-rimmed, yellow-lensed glasses standing catty-corner from series co-creator and thank-you-speech-deliverer Damon Lindelof. I suppose I always wanted to win a major award on prime-time while dressed like a Bond villain or a waiter.

At the time, one of my fellow producers turned to me and said: "The first line of your obituary was just written."

While I completely understand that my being there, even in that regrettable getup, makes my modest contribution to the Second Golden Age a matter of record -- and in the eyes of many reduces my claim to complaint -- I still marvel with some shock and horror at how much jockeying there is for the credit of being "the reason TV got good all of a sudden."

Feature film directors and screenwriters love to make

the case that it was their descent from the Olympian perches of high-stakes, high-minded, high-budget, world-class entertainment that suddenly elevated "the boob tube" into "high art." Scratch "high-budget" from the previous statement and you get the playwright's version of that argument.

The so-called "auteur showrunners" -- writer / producers who are understood to single-handedly perform short-run series miracles on basic and premium cable -- insist that it was their tenacity in forcing cowardly networks to give them the latitude to single-mindedly express their voice and vision that birthed the renaissance.

Concomitantly, the new breed of "non-writing showrunners," directors and producers who have recently gained a larger role in the upper management hierarchy of TV shows, shout from the rooftops that without their stewardship of production resources and visual storytelling, the auteur showrunners would be mere novelists.

Much to their credit, the standard-bearing Mandarins of Tiffany television in the '70s, '80s and '90s -- the Lears, Bochcos, E. Kelleys, Milchs, Carons, Whedons, and John Wellses -- mostly keep on doing what they always did so well; completely at ease with their titanic contribution and feeling no need to leap into the unseemly fray.

Ignoring their fine example, the executives chime in that -- of course -- it all happened because their maverick programming choices and game-changing strategies created environments where success made it possible to launch greater success, and take greater creative risks.

Finally, cable and satellite providers sit amused on leather chairs in the back of the room and quietly assert to one another with great certainty that they turned TV from what Hunter S. Thompson called "a cruel and shallow money trench" by offering so many channels that the demand for more and more programming eventually brought about creative critical mass.

It's the *Hamlet*/monkey argument: when the number of venues increased exponentially, so did the number of shows, and with that, the chance that, through sheer tyranny of volume, some of them would wind up being … uh … you know … good.

However fatuously expressed in press conferences and trade publication interviews, these arguments are all based on varying degrees of truth. They also ignore the less glamorous -- and less easy to claim -- cultural, technological, and social influences that created the opportunity for the Second Golden Age to arise.

My journey toward understanding the changes that led to where we are today began in 1993. After graduating with a screenwriting degree from the same school as George Lucas -- my heart's desire was the same as every other filmmaker of Generation X: to remake *Star Wars* over and over while being hailed as a creative visionary -- I blundered into a position as a junior executive in current programming and drama development at NBC. There, I got to witness not just the Viking funerals of *LA Law* and a few other still-standing, groundbreaking 10 o'clock dramas of the 1980s, but also the birth of "Must See TV"; the ongoing development of seminal shows like *Homicide: Life on the Street*, *Seinfeld*, and *Law & Order*; and the development and launch of some of the great precursors to the Second Golden Age, specifically, *E.R.* and *Friends*.

Among my most salient memories of that time is an overheard conversation between two senior broadcast executives during which one of them scratched his head and asked, "Is it just me, or is TV getting good all of a sudden?"

After two years at the network, I returned to writing -- staying in the medium I had grown to love and at which I have since worked tirelessly to achieve some proficiency. For two seasons in the mid-aughts, I not only worked as a writer and Supervising Producer of the first and second season of *Lost*, but was also, more importantly, part of a think tank of four writers (the others were Paul Dini, Jennifer Johnson, and Christian Taylor) hired by series creators JJ Abrams and Damon Lindelof to aid in the development of the series and its themes and structure while they wrote and produced the pilot episode.

That bright and shining moment aside, my bread and butter has been that of the traveling story salesman -- moving from show to show, season after season -- sometimes spending multiple years on one, often suffering the slings and arrows of early cancellation or the inevitable purges that occur in writing staffs as upper management tries to figure out the right blend of voices to enable their vision.

After putting time in brilliant-but-cancelled shows like *Boomtown*, artistically and commercially successful outings like *Medium*, popular hits like *Charmed* and *The Pretender*, limited-run basic cable series like *Helix,* cult rarities like *Jake 2.0* and *The Chronicle* -- and occasional misfires like the *Charlie's Angels* reboot and *seaQuest 2032* -- I would love to sell you the idea that the Second Golden Age of Television is the result of an army of competent journeyman craftspeople toiling endlessly and thanklessly to prop up the messianic visionaries, feature directors, empire-building absentee micromanagers, 900-pound gorillas, and network executives.

That, however, would also be fatuous and self-serving. What I have observed in 20-plus years as a member of television's middle class, and believe to be the true reasons for TV's emergence as the pre-eminent, thought-provoking, visually stimulating, character-revealing mass medium of the early twenty-first century is the result of a number of interdependent factors. All these factors are primarily external to the actual business of creating televised narrative; and none of them have anything to do with anyone's personal greatness.

Hard as it may be to admit, those of us working in television today may merely be the lucky surfers of a three-crested wave of socio-techno-psychological change.

And, believe it or not, it all starts with Meryl Streep and Dustin Hoffman.

1. IT'S NOT THE HERO'S JOURNEY, BUT THE PARENTS' DIVORCE

The most cursory glance at the pop culture zeitgeist would still provide much fuel for the argument that *Star Wars* was -- and is -- the pivotal narrative model for two generations of TV writer/producers.

While the impact of George Lucas's samurai space epic on current film and television is so deeply felt that even visiting extraterrestrials might think that Joseph Campbell's *The Hero with a Thousand Faces* as vulgarized by a frustrated race car driver from Modesto is the only true religious text of the time, I would propose that Robert Benton's 1979 film of Avery Corman's novel *Kramer vs. Kramer* is the more accurate snapshot of the formative years of today's dominant content producers.

Pound-for-pound and show-by-show, the monolithic thematic obsession of present-day narrative television can be summed up in two words: bad parenting.

In film school, I was assigned Robert B. Ray's book *A Certain Tendency of the Hollywood Cinema*. Here's the TL;DR: Every Hollywood film between 1930 and 1980 is essentially a Western focusing on either an outlaw hero or an official hero. To Ray, the film industry in those 50 years was nothing less than a vast cultural project to transpose on all genres the tropes of our national heroic narrative of manifest destiny, conquest, greatest-generation stoicism, and jingoistic machismo.

So what is the TL;DR of my first factor? Every show of the Second Golden Age of television is essentially *Kramer vs. Kramer*: a sustained exploration of the consequences of divorce -- and absent and abandoning parenting -- on the now-grown children of the first generation to experience it as a widespread social custom.

Fair or not to the parties involved, we are re-living the childhood trauma of an entire generation dramatized on television. Divorce was, quite simply, THE national narrative of the formative years of Generations X and Y in the United States. More so than Vietnam, Watergate, the AIDS epidemic, or even the fever-pitching of the Cold War by Reagan's nuclear hawks, the rising divorce rates of the 1970s and '80s touched the lives of every single American child in a profound, personal way that defined not just the way in which we would live our lives, but also the way we would use the medium of television to tell our stories.

Late-term war babies and boomers have been vilified enough for their need to claim responsibility for all that was good about the 1960s and '70s (the civil rights movement, women's lib, the sexual revolution, the counter-culture and its dismantling of the stifling "*Man in the Gray Flannel Suit*/June Cleaver" social expectations of the '50s, gay pride, and men landing on the moon) while conveniently ignoring the less-glamorous collateral effects of their activism and self-discovery (the herpes epidemic, cocaine, the rise of the extreme right wing in the '80s, a squanderous build up of the military/industrial complex that makes most YA dystopias look like YA utopias, runaway debt that will have our grandchildren striking stones to kindle the remains of their furniture for warmth, disco, and the Carter Administration).

I won't add to the vitriol, but rather point out that as divorce rates soared in the wake of the late-term war baby and boomer generation's groping attempts to define themselves in something other than the most rigidly described societal roles -- and eventually settled in the 50 percent range -- the children of divorce found themselves pioneers of an undiscovered country.

In spite of the influence of the counterculture, the self-help movement, and a growing acceptance of mental health care and psychotherapy as something other than a bitter admission of failure, American society as a whole simply lacked the methods, support mechanisms -- even the narrative tropes -- to comfort and acclimate a million-fold influx of newly minted latchkey kids to their new dual citizenship in separated, multi-variant families with often-warring authority figures. Feeling abandoned and betrayed, the children of the divorce generation -- who form the primary core of today's top-tier television writer/producers -- made the best of a situation for which few adults could provide context because they were too busy figuring it out themselves.

As these kids grew up to become content creators in their adult lives, their preferred collective narrative ceased to be victory in wartime or the conquest of a physical frontier, but rather the taming of an emotional wilderness populated by malfeasant middle-aged parent figures (usually a father, since at the time, they were more often the ones leaving home and hearth and were thus more frequently perceived as the abandoning parent). Most of the delinquent parents in this new master narrative are portrayed as inscrutably trying to reinvent themselves at the expense of their dependents.

If this seems a gross generalization, just Google the murderer's row of the most iconic dramatic series of the Second Golden Age:

- *The Sopranos* (a mobster tries to reconcile the criminal lifestyle he loves with the family he begrudges).
- *Sex and the City* (abandoned by her father at the age of five, Carrie Bradshaw finds the perfect surrogate family in her friends even as she squanders years in an on-and-off relationship with a latter-day equivalent of Daddy Warbucks).
- *Breaking Bad* (a science teacher becomes a criminal to save his family and discovers that crime was always his true love).
- *Mad Men* (the abused child of a drunk and a prostitute grows up to be a narcissistic workaholic who neglects his family).
- *Lost* (every character is an abandoned child trying to remake him/herself in a deserted island where no one knows their true past).
- *Orange Is the New Black* (a catalogued exhibition of birth mothers extending their abusive pasts to their children and jailed abuse survivors seeking surrogate mothers behind bars).

- *House MD* (a brilliant but narcissistic drug addict abuses his surrogate wife and children in the workplace).
- *Grey's Anatomy* (The narcissistic workaholic children of narcissistic workaholic parents wreak endless emotional havoc on one another while excelling in the workplace).
- *True Detective* (a philandering cop who neglects his family finds the platonic definition of love in a nihilistic, workaholic partner overcompensating for the tragic loss of his own wife and daughter).
- *The Good Wife* (a case study in the preservation of a marriage for the sake of appearances).
- *Sons of Anarchy* (*Hamlet* in a biker gang).
- *Six Feet Under* (a primer on the neglected children of children of abuse -- one whose inciting event is the ultimate act of abandonment by a father).
- *Orphan Black* (in which not one but a whole gaggle of Tatiana Maslanys learn how dangerous it is to have been raised by strangers).
- *The Shield* (an amoral philandering cop excuses his ruthless pursuit of his evil moral code by convincing himself that it's all to protect the family he chronically neglects).
- 24 (Jack Bauer tragically loses his family and can never love again for serving the stars-and-stripes -- a vocation that eventually brings him into conflict with his own powerful but corrupt father and catamitic younger brother).
- *Battlestar Galactica* (the spurned children of humanity form a weird monotheistic cult and then come back to burn down their parents' home with nuclear weapons).

- *The Wire* (a longitudinal study of an entire generation's abandonment by an uncaring patriarchy).

And here's the kicker: the handful of shows of the era that are not about bad parenting are generally so inversely proportional in their correction (*Friday Night Lights* and *Parenthood*, each a celebration of the world's hardest working, most self-improving parents, and *The West Wing*, a fantasy in which the world's ultimate patriarch is an almost preternaturally moral man who actually grapples with the idea of compromise) that they come off as the exceptions that prove the rule.

The Second Golden Age of television owes much of its existence to the Golden Age of American Divorce... and my generation's final reckoning with our parents may just lie in cursing them with decades of recriminatory reruns depicting their perceived sins.

Which leads to the second factor, which has something to do with what all those latchkey kids were doing in front of the television in the years immediately following 1984.

2. MTV -- BUT NOT IN THE WAY YOU THINK

In many media-savvy people, the mere mention of "MTV" triggers Pavlov-like the addition of the suffix "-style editing." The conventional wisdom among many is that MTV's historical legacy to the medium is the trickle-down of the rapid-fire editing style of music video to mass-produced narrative entertainment.

The story that usually accompanies this argument goes something like this: "When Brandon Tartikoff first proposed the kernel that became *Miami Vice*, he merely wrote down the words 'MTV COPS' on a cocktail napkin."

While the role of MTV in introducing a faster-paced visual literacy to the general population, especially in the 1980s, cannot be denied, one can also argue that Pablo Ferro had already been cutting that way since the '60s -- and so were the makers of *Help, A Hard Day's Night, The Monkees,* and pretty much every commercial director and avant-garde filmmaker in existence. So while MTV may have expedited the arrival of a certain style and fashion to the suburbs, style and fashion have -- historically -- always found their way there in some other way or another (just ask Elvis Presley, the Beatles, the Sex Pistols, and Halston). The true influence of MTV on the Second Golden Age is the result of something much subtler -- yet far, far more subversive.

Having an entire generation of future television show creators grow up on a turbocharged diet of high-density chunks of five minute narrative vignettes -- one-after-the-other-all-day-long, all of them wildly varying in genre, all of them wildly experimental in ways once reserved for the art house -- created in the collective unconscious a vast and widely shared tolerance for genre-bending in narrative.

The vernacular of modern television -- in which cop shows routinely trade in the tropes of procedurals as well as horror movies, or large segments of a show that deals in flash-backs and flash-forwards airs on network television with non-anglophone characters and subtitles, or in which the "musical episode" is not only a curiosity, but, in some cases, an ongoing gesture, or a series that plays entirely in real time with elements of soap opera, action thriller, and police procedural all showing simultaneously on multiple split screens, or in which individual seasons of a show are completely different from previous seasons of the same show, sharing only a title, cast, an aesthetic, and certain thematic preoccupations -- would never have existed without MTV.

After 50-plus years of complacently doling out a tightly regimented school lunch tray of cop / doctor / lawyer / family / sitcom, the dawn of the Second Golden Age marks the point when television suddenly -- and seemingly collectively -- decided that trans-textual promiscuity was a far more satisfying endeavor than the pursuit of haiku-like perfection in the extant formats. This aesthetic shift also dovetails nicely with the promotion to power in the medium of an entire generation of creators whose formative years consisted of obsessively consuming a single channel in which it was possible to go from Godley & Creme to Derek Jarman to David Fincher in a span of minutes: an experience also shared by the audience then rising as the desirable demographic target for new shows.

Imagine an entire crop of impressionable minds watching one monolithic network where the shows changed genre at a speed unthinkable in any previous form of broadcasting. From kitchen sink drama (Madonna's "Papa Don't Preach" and Donna Summer's "She Works Hard for the Money") to homoerotic Indiana Jones--style action-adventure (Duran Duran's "Hungry Like the Wolf"), to Lou Reed singing about transvestites, to raunchy, socially reprehensible comedy (let's say John Parr's "Naughty, Naughty"), to a piece of pop-art directed by Andy Warhol (The Cars's "Hello Again"), to a quasi-druidic tone-poem in which a member of Monty Python was tortured by demons (Iron Maiden's "Can I Play with Madness"), to a Talking Heads clip inspired by the outsider art of Reverend Howard Finster, and a glossy Hollywood musical that just happened to feature Michael Jackson and a cast of line-dancing zombies, MTV was that network, and then some.

By simultaneously being the world's top provider of pop music -- the common tongue of worldwide youth culture -- and wedding that to a voraciously (indeed, almost viciously) derivative visual aesthetic that drew much of its energy from the recycling and remixing of anything and everything in the culture, MTV rewired the brains of an entire generation to accept the possibility that narrative could span a multiplicity genres within an integrated whole.

In a feat of mental engineering unprecedented in its speed and scope -- a nation-sized experiment that puts the brainwashers of *The Manchurian Candidate* to shame -- MTV facilitated in an entire population a willingness to experiment, first as consumers, and later as creators, with a gonzo fluidity of storytelling and content that echoes in even the most high-minded and erudite of the current age's narrative offerings.

There's a reason why *Lost* was a soap opera, and a sci-fi show, and a spy thriller, and a romantic melodrama, and an occasional police procedural, and a hospital drama, and a wacky comedy about an accidental millionaire, and a paranoid conspiracy thriller that unfolded in a non-linear collage of flash-backs, flash-forwards and flash sideways... and there's also a reason why *Lost*, as insane as it sounds in hindsight, is not a mere outlier, but very much emblematic of the style and substance of the Second Golden Era of Television: it was just like watching MTV in the 1980s.

But the single most important of the three factors that caused television to "get good" starting in the early to mid-'90s, and brought it to a great blossoming of experimentation and excellence at the dawn of the millennium -- the one that ties all of the above together -- is the one that gets most easily lost in the land grab for the glory.

In the end, it was technology that brought us all to the Promised Land.

3. THE RISE OF DIGITAL, NON-LINEAR FILMMAKING

When you buy a laptop -- or even a smartphone -- it will usually include some kind of imaging and editing software, allowing you to take videos, shuffle scenes around, add titles, change the colors, add some filters, maybe a little CGI animation, and then email the entire Kubrickian enterprise to your next of kin. Having grown up in the analog era of filmmaking, I find this a staggering idea on the same level as the notion that the average air conditioning thermostat installed in a new house today carries within it more computing power than the Apollo 11 space capsule.

The first time I walked into a professional postproduction suite was in 1993. In my capacity as an NBC executive, I visited the offices of *seaQuest DSV* -- a series that not only boasted the first dedicated, in-house, computer-generated visual effects company for a television series (Steven Spielberg's Amblin Imaging) but was also my first encounter with non-linear, non-destructive editing. Sitting alone in a corner by several humming Lightworks workstations -- and half-draped in a tarp like a hobbled mechanical pterodactyl -- was an old-school Moviola film-editing machine.

That was the moment I realized the revolution was being televised.

In the pre-digital era, there simply was no physical way TV could compete with the quality of the visual image on feature films. The writing, shooting, and postproduction schedules -- which persist almost unchanged to this day -- simply did not allow a great deal of visual variety in filming, or experimentation in the editing and finishing of the TV product.

Consider a relatively modestly budgeted feature film of the 1980s -- say, Paul Verhoeven's 1987 *RoboCop*. Made for $13 million, the film was planned for a year before the cameras rolled for two and a half months between August and October of 1986. Reshoots were performed in January of the following year. The film was released in July 1987 after nine months of postproduction.

A similarly themed television series of the same vintage -- *Max Headroom* -- had to deliver competitive visuals on roughly one-tenth of that budget with eight days of planning, eight days of shooting, and less than a month of editing, scoring, and visual effects production per episode: a punishing grind that most TV programs have to maintain week in and week out to make their air dates and stay on budget.

A TV company usually rented one 35-millimeter film camera (with an occasional second if you had a clever line producer with a keen eye toward maximizing equipment rental budgets). In this environment, even an experienced crew in a soundstage was severely hampered in the number of camera set-ups they could light and capture in a single day. TV crews barely had time to cover all the angles necessary to capture the bare necessities: the truly eye-popping shots were few and far between.

Similarly, analog postproduction was a taxing -- and sometimes nigh-artisanal -- process. Editors working on film or video found their ability to deliver anything beyond the most workmanlike results severely constrained: every change to the material was "destructive" -- requiring the undoing of everything around it without the simple convenience of a "redo" button. In the 1950s and '60s, an editor's assistant literally had to pull the work print apart and reassemble the pieces with splicing tape to address a note. In the 1970s and '80s, the process required the cumbersome overdubbing of edits from two separate tape decks onto a third -- effectively erasing all the previous work.

Additionally, every fade, split-screen, and wipe -- or simple color correction, and the modest reframing or blow-ups of shots: operations that any eight-year-old can perform in seconds on iMovie today -- had to be executed separately in a lab and took a major toll on the series budget. There was no ability to "drag and drop" a transition into a timeline just to see whether it would work or not. Special effects shots had to be planned to the frame and were not only severely limited, but also recycled from episode to episode (watch any hour of the original *Star Trek* and count how many times you see the same flyby of the Enterprise).

Truly, this was the equivalent of writing a script on a typewriter, and making revisions with onion skin paper, scissors, and Elmer's glue. It wasn't a lack of ideas or desire to improve the medium that kept television from greatness, but rather the physical limitations of the one mode of production. Making changes and experimenting with the product took a lot of time and cost a lot of money -- and time and money were the two things that were always in short supply.

In the early '90s, however, non-linear, non-destructive editing systems -- most of them less powerful than the stock version of iMovie bundled for free with your average

Mac today -- began to appear in TV postproduction. The change was swift and astonishing. Five years down the line, it became rare to find a film school graduate who had edited on film. Less than eight years later, the very medium was reborn.

How did it happen? With non-linear/non-destructive editing, writer/producers gained the ability to see the assembled work faster. They were able to spend more time thinking the material through, seeing results in real time, and demanding more footage to work with... as well as writing more complicated scripts to accommodate the growing visual palette promised by advancing technology. With non-linear/non-destructive technology, editing went from a mere assembly of a limited set of elements to a final rewrite with the benefit of endless do-overs.

Less than a decade later, the arrival of relatively cheap high-definition digital cameras became the second-stage rocket of television's ascent. With the expense of raw film stock and camera rentals no longer a drain on budgets (broadcast-quality video is now shootable on an off-the-shelf DSLR camera) the number of setups, angles, and scenes has increased exponentially. It's a simple matter of ratios: we can now capture more at lesser effort and expense, allowing more scenes to be shot per day in a more visually dynamic way.

So while the amount of time we have to do our work hasn't changed -- seven- to eight-day shooting schedules, 13 to 22 episodes a year, network pilots in January, fall season premieres in September -- the amount of work that can be done in that time, and our ability to indulge and render what's in our minds, has changed by orders of magnitude. Consider this example: the split-screen storytelling technique used in 24 would have taken weeks per individual episode to accomplish in the '70s using optical printers -- and the amount of footage necessary to get the number of shots would have been cost-prohibitive. Simply, the style of 24 was not physically achievable in the '70s, where today, multiple HD cameras, non-linear editing and digital post production accomplish in a short span of time what was once untenable.

These advances in technology ultimately created a cost-effective production infrastructure that today allows established networks to experiment with shows that might not have lasted before. *That Friday Night Lights* was allowed five excellent seasons in the aughts under a co-production deal between NBC and DirectTV, while the similarly themed *Against the Grain* was cancelled after two months on NBC primetime in the 1990s, is a reasonable example. The same advances gave basic cable networks the freedom to commission original work to fill their airwaves at budgets that permit smaller and more narrowly defined audiences to produce the kind of advertising revenue that keeps shows on the air -- and have also freed pay cable networks to double-down on their own ambitions.

Where once there was *Supermarket Sweep* and *Check it Out!* there is now *Rectify* and *Louie*. Where once there was *First and Ten* and *Dream On*, there now is *Game of Thrones* and *Girls*. Where once there was the much-mocked CableACE Award, there are now Emmy sweeps that shame the once-thought-invincible broadcast networks. Technology created the opportunity to make new types of shows cheaply, the 500-channel universe seized on the opportunity, and the deluge of creative competition lifted everyone to a new level of ambition and competence.

The TV-making monkeys weren't just given typewriters -- they happened upon a socio-cultural-technological monolith, and they evolved and multiplied accordingly.

CONCLUSION: "GET OFF THE STAGE, FATBOY!"
My own personal relationship to the "Second Golden Age of Television" up until now can best be summed up in two career-defining events. On the night *Lost* won the Best Drama Series Emmy, we were quickly hustled to a back-room photo gallery along with the series cast. While technically not the recipients of the award, cast members are nonetheless invited onto stage and attendant press to spare the viewing public the dystelegenic sight of pasty, monastic scribes who seldom see the light of day, strutting their hour upon the stage after some very unfortunate sartorial decisions.

In this room, a large crowd of photographers stood on tiered risers while the producers, writers, and cast posed on a small stage. The reporters, as remains their custom, shouted loudly and endlessly for their subjects to turn toward them so that they could get the best possible picture.

After a while, we handed off the trophies to the cast so they could pose with them. For a moment I found myself slipping into something of a stunned reverie and wandering in front of the stage in a haze of flashbulb lights and loud, demanding voices. My fugue was broken by a shrill shriek from one of the photographers:

"GET OFF THE STAGE, FATBOY, YOU'RE IN MY SHOT OF EVANGELINE!"

Duly reminded of my true place in the entertainment-industrial complex, I meekly stepped out of the way and let the photogs get their pictures of our leading lady. Seven days later, I drove to my parents' house and gave them the trophy -- not for any disdain for the Academy or what it represents, but because they paid for me to go to film school: and because the explosive change I have seen in my time in the industry is a constant reminder that it is the forward movement of creativity that earns awards, not a dwelling on what worked in the past.

My second career-defining event was the 12-episode run of *The Middleman*, a television series I created and executive produced for the ABC Family cable network in 2008. A deeply -- almost ridiculously -- idiosyncratic mashup of the popular culture of my youth with my adult desire to express a message of optimism, cooperation, and common decency, *The Middleman* was a latter-day sci-fi-superhero-comedy produced on a budget only slightly higher than that of *Max Headroom* 20 years earlier.

While not a commercial success, the series allowed me to marshal a kind-hearted group of mostly like-minded writers and artists to express something I never would have had the opportunity had I been born in the 1940s or '50s and worked in anything other than the TV medium as it stands today. Six years since, *The Middleman* continues to live in DVDs and various other download services, where its small, but delightful and devoted, cult audience will presumably continue to enjoy it and recommend it to their own friends.

To be one of what is still a very small number of artists working in this mass medium is a privilege -- a collusion of hard work and life-changing luck for which I will always be grateful. To be able to work the medium on so personal a scale as I have had the opportunity: to create something that, if not world-changing, at least presented me with the opportunity to stand before a planet-sized audience, yell "hello!" and know that the statement will linger in a meaningful way rather than to vanish into the electronic ether -- that, to me, is the true Golden Age.

While there will always be those who claim that their own specific contribution was the pivot for the descent of quality upon the medium, the memory I carry with me through my own career is that many of us who love television -- regardless of where we came from or have been -- were given a massive socio-technological boon and rose to the occasion. We took advantage of a newfound technological flexibility to explore our own cultural proclivities and societal anxieties. Having experienced these technological and artistic changes in real time -- as a viewer, then a network executive, and currently a creator -- I know that the difference between what was possible in 1987, versus what was possible in 1993, versus what is possible today is comparable to waking up one morning with the ability to turn off gravity and truly fly.

WHY I WEAR A FUNNY HAT

Published privately in June of 2000, as part of a primer for students graduating from Carnegie Mellon University's Playwriting program.

If you expect me to tell you how to get an agent, turn to the next article. Substitute the words "job," "audition," and "career" into the past sentence if you need any further clarification. Chances are that you will not get an agent/job/audition/career in the exact same way as anyone else. After six years in the entertainment industry -- two as a television executive and four as a writer -- the only thing I know with absolute certainty is that that no one can tell you exactly how to make the journey.

Showbiz is like a small village without roads. Your destination is always in sight, but you have to define your own path. I don't have the "magic ticket"... and anyone who says they do is more interested in your money than your career. What I have to offer is advice. Now, I'm no monument to truth, justice and the American Way (my best friends will gladly tell you that I am deeply flawed and seldom return calls on time) but the following are the ideals I strive for as I try to negotiate a life in the entertainment industry.

1. Be In It for the Long Haul

No two expressions (both usually spoken by the cocky

and clueless) piss me off more than "I'm going to give it a year, to see if I can make it," and "I just finished my first script, and I know it's going to sell for a million bucks." Entering this industry to make a quick score is like becoming a doctor because you like golf. My six years in the industry and are a drop in the cosmic bucket. To truly succeed, I know that I have to sustain a level of success and personal happiness for decades to come. To quote Frank Herbert's *Dune*: "God created [the planet] Arrakis to test the faithful." The same applies to showbiz. Nowhere else will you find the amount of madness, rage, and abuse you encounter as a professional in this industry... but the rewards are certainly worth it. Your capacity to succeed depends on your ability to survive. Your ability to survive depends on whether you can consistently deliver quality work for a sustained period of time. You may succeed at an early age. You may succeed later in life. You may not succeed at all... but you won't know unless you make a commitment for the long haul.

2. Practice Your Craft Diligently

Ask yourself: Am I ready to be a professional writer? I guarantee that the point when you think you have written enough is the beginning of your quest, not the end. Don't believe for a second that your last (or only) script is your best and entitles you to success. It is not, it does not, and, more often than not, it will not. If you have just completed a script, then write another one, then another, and another. Study other people's scripts and films... and know that when you do, you may feel angry because you feel you can and have done better. Do everything you can to work past that anger and use it to your advantage. Don't whine: write an objective, analytical essay in which you explain to yourself why what you have seen others do doesn't work. Developing the analytical tools to judge your own work and that of others is as much a part of being a scriptwriter as to writing scripts. Ultimately, the more experience you acquire, the more you should come understand your own lack of mastery: there's always more to be learned, and there's nothing you can do that cannot be made better.

3.   Learn When to Let Go

A central principle in the Buddhist way of life is that all misery stems from attachment. Part of mastering a craft is knowing when you have learned everything there is to learn from a project. Don't mistake practicing your craft diligently with obsessing over a single piece of work for years on end. Even after you've done all you can to make your work the best it can be, you may still learn that it's not the script that's going to land you the million-dollar development deal. Take what you have learned and use it to make the next script better: your career is about sustained improvement over an extended period of time. Sometimes you will know it's time to let go when you feel like you're hitting your head with a two-by-four. Sometimes, you will merely sense that you are working much too hard to make something work when deep down inside you know that it doesn't. This philosophy applies to scripts, scenes, lines, and characters: you sometimes have to abandon the things you love in order to grow. You will have many children -- some will win Nobel Prizes, some will wind up hawking fries at McDonald's. Learn to live with that.

4.   If You Build It They Will Come

You are a writer, but no one is paying you to write. Does

that make you any less of a writer? If no one is seeking to employ or represent you, then you have to motivate yourself to continue writing and create a venue for yourself (and by the way, do not, under any circumstance, write someone else's stories if you are not getting paid -- you may not be employed, but working for free is just plain unprofessional). Consider this: Los Angeles is full of small theaters and performance spaces, and the tools of film-making are readily available to anyone wily enough to recognize where to find them. There are more independent festivals for both plays and short films than I can count. If you are not creating for money, create for your own personal growth. Write and produce a play or a short film -- promote and nurture them as you would if you were getting paid. Practice your craft and expand your horizons: eventually someone will take notice.

5. Create a Community

You may recognize this VERY loose paraphrase of Ezekiel 25:17 from either the Bible or the film *Pulp Fiction*:

> *"The path of the righteous man is beset on all sides by the iniquities of the selfish and the tyranny of evil men. Blessed is he who, in the name of charity and good will, shepherds the weak through the valley of darkness, for he is truly his brother's keeper and the finder of lost children. And I will strike down upon thee with great vengeance and furious anger those who attempt to poison and destroy my brother. And you will know my name is THE LORD when I lay my vengeance upon you."*

Now, I'm neither a religious person, nor am I about to get medieval on your ass. This quote is simply as close a metaphor for the entertainment industry as I can imagine. If you want to succeed in a business that eats its young and (on a good day) does business with lead-pipe cruelty, you may want to consider practicing the virtues of charity, kindness, and good will. If you can help someone you know to get a job, do it. If you believe in a friend's talent, give them the best feedback you can and help them to advance their cause by any means at your disposal. Rejoice in your friends' successes and comfort them in their failures. Be honest but kind, and try to create good will wherever you can. Both you and your friends need all the help you can get. Don't seek power, seek trust. Sometimes you will be the righteous man. Sometimes you will be the shepherd. Sometimes you will be the weak. Learn to live with the tenuous nature of success and avoid embodying the iniquities of the selfish and the tyranny of evil men... for all the obvious reasons, not the least of which is the striking down with great vengeance thing. The rarest commodities in this industry are not good ideas, they are loyalty, friendship, and community. Success is fleeting, failure is painful, and creation is a difficult collaborative art. It is best to go through all of these with people you love and trust.

6. Stay Healthy

A working TV writer spends six to 15 hours a day in a conference room eating really bad take-out food. Concurrently, the biggest occupational hazards are obesity, a bad back, and depression. Make the time to keep yourself fit on all fronts. Don't take any shortcuts, and don't buy into the bulldada that to be successful creatively you have to be a compulsive workaholic with dark thoughts, a taste for scotch, and a tortured soul. Working diligently and working yourself to death are two completely different animals. The happier you are, the more creative you will be. It's that simple... and for God's sake, man, leave all that all that "black turtleneck-wearing Rimbaud Romantic Poseur die young" crap back in college where it belongs. Entertaining America is a job for strong minds and healthy bodies. You can be as neurotic, quirky, and unique as you want, but you won't have much of a chance to show it to the world if you keel over dead of a heart attack, commit suicide, or drink yourself into oblivion.

The bad and beautiful of the entertainment industry both stem from its lack of structure. There are many ways to find success, fortune and fulfillment. You may achieve your goals by learning to effectively market yourself, you may do it by attending seminars and talks, you may write a million-dollar spec the first time out... and you may get to exactly where you want to be only to learn that it is not everything you imagined. None of these are wrong, but what that means is that in the end you must measure success through a standard of your own making.

You will have many bosses -- some of them will be good and decent people who will nurture your talent. Others will be depraved fuckwads who get their jollies from playing stickball with your guts. Learn what each of them does well, because one of the cruel injustices of the universe is that even the sick and evil can have talent and succeed. When your time comes, treat your own charges in the way you would prefer to be treated -- but do not let anyone be the final authority on your success and ability. Relying solely on the opinions of authority figures for your self esteem is the path to insanity. In the end, your standard of success has to include not only your professional standing, but also your mental, physical and spiritual well-being.

I have a funny hat. My wife-to-be bought it at Disneyland. It's a big felt thing in the shape of Mickey Mouse's hand. The hat reminds me that I live in a tiny village created entirely out of cloth by a very small community of people out of which only a few can be trusted to be honest, forthright and worthy of influencing my self-esteem. While I love writing for television, take it tremendously seriously, and hope and plan to do it for the rest of my life, the silly hat is what I call a "perspective preservation device." It reminds me that happiness is the wrong price to pay for being an artist and a craftsman. As much as I want to succeed by the standards of the industry, I am not about to offer my respect for the craft of writing, my desire to do my best work, or my silly hat in trade.

It's just too good a hat.

THE CAUTIONARY TALE OF THE BIOMORPHIC CHAODAI SIDEARM

Originally published December 4, 2004, on Livejournal.

T his is a long a long and rambling story -- but it does have a point... so bear with me, and settle down... Uncle Javi is going to spin a yarn of obsession, lust, and redemption.

A few years ago, the Sci-Fi Channel ran a show called *Sci-Ography*, kind of a *VH1: Behind the Music* for science fiction TV shows. I found the first few episodes, on *Quantum Leap* and *Galactica,* pretty cool and dishy.

Then the call came in -- did I want to be interviewed for the episode of *Sci-Ography* tracking the rise and fall -- or was it the fall, fall, and then even greater fall of *seaQuest DSV*?

Absolutely not.

At the time I felt like I had already spent an inordinately large amount of my time and energy answering for the sins of *seaQuest DSV*. I was a network series executive on the show for its first two years and a staff writer during its final season, when it was retitled *seaQuest 2032.*

Here's a quick metaphorical primer on what network and studio executives do. The network is a department store: they decide what kind of merchandise they want to put on their windows and then pay to subcontract the manufacture of that merchandise to the writers and producers. The studio is simultaneously the bank that lends the writers and producers whatever additional monies they may need to make the product -- hoping their profits on the back end will make up for the deficit -- and also the factory where the merchandise is made.

The studio executive is the person who makes sure that the people on the factory floor -- the writers, directors, actors -- have everything they need to make the merchandise. The network executive is the guy who goes down to the factory floor to make sure the show being made is the one the network was sold, and tries to offer guidance on how the show may best meet the needs of the network.

At the age of 23, I was that last guy -- on a sci-fi show no less. Dreams do come true.

That much said, make no mistake, *seaQuest DSV* was a sad, sad example of television gone horribly wrong. It is a textbook case of what happens when too many talented people throw way too much good money after bad.

Part of me wishes the show could be remembered as the kind of campy, *Buck Rogers*-eque misfire that amuses people to no end for years and causes geeks like me to write rambling essays of fondly snide praise and plunk down wads of cash for a set of DVDs laughably titled "the complete epic series..."

Nope.

It should have been great. Executive Producer Steven Spielberg! Starring Academy Award Nominee Roy

Scheider! A pilot directed by Irvin-*The Empire Strikes Back*-freakin'-Kershner! But the fact that we aren't watching the tenth season of *seaQuest DSV* today, or checking out the triumphant launch of the spin-off series *seaQuest: Voyager*, or plunking down $15.00 to see *seaQuest 2 -- The Wrath of the Regulator* at the local multiplex, pretty much says it all.

seaQuest DSV premiered to the highest ratings for any drama in the history of primetime... and then steadily declined over the course two and a half seasons, a show kept on life support by massive infusions of promotional money, and network support, and the desire to appease Steven Spielberg -- even though he had all but disowned the show by the end of its first season. I was one of the people providing and advocating for that support.

For me, *seaQuest DSV* was like that abusive, drama vampire relationship everyone has at least once in their life (or which *Star Trek* fans have had with the franchise for the past 10 years, take your pick). You think it can be better, you want it to get better, you hope that it will heal, and you believe you have the power to make it whole -- even though the tear-stained trail of boiled bunnies, sugar-filled gas tanks, and baguette-hurling altercations that get you banned from restaurants screams otherwise.

I did everything I could within my meager place as a junior network *apparatchik* -- not only was I very young, I was straight out of grad school and very eager to make my mark by giving TONS of notes and suggestions: exactly the kind of naive and wet-behind-the-ears young person Harlan Ellison rants about having to suffer -- to try and make this show work. I wanted to be part of something that could leave behind a *Star Trek*-like legacy. I refused to believe that with all that money and talent, the show couldn't just snap out of it and, for the sweet love of

Sparky Schultz's pen, just be FREAKIN' GOOD!

But it just wasn't to be -- that elusive alchemy that makes good shows good just didn't rear it's mystical little head this time.

How much could a young, naïve network executive with not a lot of power do in a situation like this? A lot, it turns out. I battled the NBC on-air promo department for more air time, even though they regularly berated me because the show did not have promotable stories. I travelled to the show's production facility in Orlando, Florida and produced a series of promotional behind-the-scenes documentaries myself. I tried to lure writers from *Star Trek* -- both *The Next Generation* and *Deep Space Nine* -- to leave their jobs and help "save" *seaQuest DSV*. I butted heads with angry fans during the infancy of web fandom (actually, that's not true, I made a game effort of being a peace maker, opened a door for fans to send me their opinions of the show and wound up in the crossfire of a letter writing campaign that wanted Roy Scheider to be given creative control over the series and the wrath of the network's PR department, who felt that by responding, I had made it possible for a small group of rabid fans to actually have a voice) and made myself the butt of Usenet posters for years thereafter... and for what?

Well... in hindsight that dysfunctional attachment to *seaQuest DSV* was the thing that started my writing career. By the time the showrunner offered to bring me in as a staff writer if the show got picked up for its third season (he probably got sick of listening to all my lame story ideas during conference calls -- and God bless him for that -- I truly am eternally grateful) I don't think anyone expected that season to come.

What makes me say that? Well...

The second season finale ended with seaQuest -- the titular submarine -- destroyed, most of the crew dead and drowned -- and the only three members of the ensemble who didn't appear to have been killed by a barrier mine were bobbing in a raft in the open water...

Oh, and did I mention that this all took place on the alien planet of "Hyberion?"

That's right -- not only did they blow up the damn ship -- they did it on another freakin' world (and one whose name looked like a typo, no less).

Additionally, NBC was actively developing another sci-fi/action adventure show to take the place of *seaQuest DSV* -- and I knew this. I was on the inside!

Nevertheless, I not only agreed to take the staff writer job on this moribund golem of a series, I also diligently went about the task of making it the worst-kept secret in Hollywood that I was perfectly willing to ditch a promising career at the network in order to go work on a show that had become an industry punchline: something from which it would have taken years to recover had I truly wanted a long-term career in the executive ranks.

Mercifully, God has a sense of humor. The show with which NBC intended to replace *seaQuest DSV* was called *Rolling Thunder:* the rollicking, stand-up-and-cheer saga of a super secret elite government crimefighting unit...

That drove around in monster trucks.

Yep. Monster-truck-drivin' secret agents.

Because there is no better way of sneakin' up on the baddies than in a MONSTER FARGIN' TRUCK!

That's how *seaQuest DSV* got its third season (and I got my first writing gig): not by being good, but by just not being as godawful as the next guy.

My first episode was an unmitigated disaster. It

was a heart-warming yarn about a disaster onboard an underwater train that inexplicably travelled from San Francisco Bay to Beijing (an inland city -- oh, and the area through which the train travelled is known as the "Ring of Fire," the most actively volcanic region of the Pacific Ocean floor -- the best place in the world to put an underwater train, right?).

Right now, you would be correct to assume that the only thing that could make this worse would be the inclusion of a semi-nude massage scene and a dance sequence.

Oh... wait... it had those too.

I am not exactly sure of the reason why those things were put in, but I know the how. It was my failure to appropriately render the story in the first place that led to the inclusion of all that scientific inaccuracy, T&A, and bad dancing. I take full responsibility, not for coming up with that crap, but for creating the vacuum which it filled.

The second episode I worked on, co-written with a fine writer who became a mentor and great friend to me over the years, was much better. My third and final episode, titled *Weapons of War,* is -- to this day -- one of my favorite scripts.

Basically, the show was all but cancelled, dead in the water -- and everyone knew it. I, however, had a master plan to introduce a new series regular -- a defector from an evil empire that would serve as a menace through the rest of the season. The crew of seaQuest would finally have their memorable antagonist -- their Klingons -- and I was given permission to create this evil race that would revitalize the franchise...

Primarily because the show was dead, and this was the last episode in the order, and no one cared anymore. Why not let the delusional kid have his fun?

So I was left to my own devices to write the eppie... and it was shot. And the new character -- Lt. Heiko Kimura of the Chaodai -- was kick-ass as played by the lovely, talented, and sexy Julia Nickson. She was Seven-of-Nine years before Seven-of-Nine was a glint in Brannon Braga's eye (down to the skin-tight silver suit) -- a cybernetically enhanced tush-whipping polyglot (for geek appeal) who could pilot her ultra-sleek subfighter by jacking in with her MIND!

And she had this cool, biomorphic sidearm.

Oh, yeah. This was SO gonna bring *seaQuest* back from the brink!

Of course, *seaQuest 2032* was cancelled and *Weapons of War* aired several months later in the West Coast as filler after a baseball game. Years later it re-ran on the Sci-Fi Channel. I can probably count the number of people who ever saw this episode with my fingers and toes.

Thus, *seaQuest* was finally laid to rest... and I wrote the last episode ever. I may have even put the last nail on the coffin... I mean, I can't say that I killed it, but I sure as hell held its hand -- praying for its survival even as the heart monitor rang with that unminstakable BEEEEEEP that everyone knows as the telltale sign that the Grim Reaper's come a-knockin'.

The sets were struck. The cast scattered. The props and costumes were auctioned off at Universal Studios in Orlando, Florida, where the show was filmed.

And so, the relationship ended. Not because I finally removed my head from my sigmoid orifice and realized that my metaphorical televisual girlfriend was loony-bananas -- but because she was killed by the hundred-mile-an-hour jacknifing-and-exploding fuel tanker also known as ratings failure.

But I wanted something to remember her by. I wanted Kimura's cool biomorphic gun. Of course, I missed the prop auction in Florida -- my agent, may God bless his soul, actually got me another paying gig (something few of us expected to happen, considering that my sole credit was a show that had been affectionately nicknamed "voyage to the bottom of the ratings").

So I moved on. I stopped taking it upon myself to answer for the many transgressions of *seaQuest DSV* and *2032*. I made the realization that the show was never mine in any way... that I was just a misguided fan with a lot more access than the average bear... and what was it that I saw in her in the first place? I mean -- there were so many other, better shows out there, and eventually, I even got the chance to work on some of them...

And I turned down the opportunity to talk publicly about the show on *Sci-Ography*.

Because, as Lou Gramm of Foreigner said so wisely during the '80s: "that was yesterday, now it's over and done."

I saw Kimura's raygun several years after the cancellation of *seaQuest* in an "online prop museum." Desperate for a souvenir of what I still thought to be my finest hour of television, I offered the guy twelve hundred dollars for that worthless hunk of fiberglass -- I mean, he'd be a fool to turn that kind of money down, right? And I was willing to bust the bank for one touch, just one last caress from the old girl...

He turned me down.

A few years later, my wife -- trying to surprise me for my thirtieth birthday -- contacted the guy with another offer to buy Kimura's sidearm. This time he didn't even write her back.

Dude must have thought we were a pair of deranged Chaodai weapon stalkers.

Then, last year, as I toiled on *Jake 2.0*, on my tenth year as a professional working in the television industry -- my eighth as a writer, and now a Supervising Producer as well -- I learned something magical.

There were actually several versions of Kimura's gun, and the "Hero Prop" -- the one with the battery-powered sequential LED display, not the one in the online prop museum, but a BETTER one -- existed out there...

And it was up for auction at a movie memorabilia house here in LA.

It was a harrowing week. I couldn't take time off from *Jake 2.0* to go to the auction because the show was behind schedule and we needed all hands on deck. But the auction was live on eBay -- and my wife, may she receive blessings from Jesus, Buddha and the Wizard of Oz -- sat online through the entire auction until that lot came up...

And she got it.

Of course, we were the only bidders -- and we paid a third of what I had offered for it years before. Only one man wanted that worthless hunk of fiberglass.

Now it sits on display in a clear plastic box in a well-trafficked but not necessarily privileged corner of our home. I take it out on occasion and turn on the LED display -- and I won't lie to you, I sometimes strike my best Gunkata pose with it while looking at a mirror. I'm not above copping to that...

And I swear that if you get near enough, if you touch your nose to that worn, silver-spray painted fiberglass, you may just catch yourself a whiff of the sweet, sweet smell of closure.

Of course, if NBC ever decides to bring back *seaQuest DSV* with a radical *Battlestar Galactica*-style reimagining of the concept, I do have some ideas I have been working on...

SUBMITTED FOR YOUR APPROVAL

Originally published March 16 and 17, 2006 on Livejournal.

PART ONE

The biggest fallacy I encounter regarding the entertainment industry is that a job here can be acquired through the same channels as in any other industry. Now, I'm not going to try to sell you on the horsepucky that what we do is so rarefied that it cannot be understood. If anything, showbiz is a lot easier to understand than, say, investment banking, or particle physics -- or the correct circumstances under which you should be honest when asked if a person looks fat in an outfit -- but it does have its rituals... and as with any human endeavor with rituals, getting them wrong can mean eternal banishment... or worse, unemployment.

On several occasions, people have said to me "I want to be a writer and I'd like to submit a script." My answer to that is invariably "to whom?"

The perception remains widely held among knowledgeable adults who should definitely know better that the entertainment industry is this monolithic edifice with a film, television, video game and vaudeville department. All one has to do is "submit" a script and it will be duly considered.

(This is second only to the equally widely held belief

that ALL TV writers hang out with each other -- more than once I have found myself in the company of people who just assume I'm best friends with Aaron Sorkin/ Joss Whedon/Alan Ball -- as if there's a club where we all write our scripts, eat our meals, and then hit the treadmills together before we all collectively go for a *schvitz*... frankly, it's too bad there isn't such a place, I could use a good *schvitz*, but I digress...)

Obviously, that is not the case.

So let's go through the steps of getting a job as a writer in the entertainment industry... from somebody who is currently trying to get a job there!

First of all, you <u>need</u> an agent.

Why do you <u>need</u> an agent? A middleman to "submit" your work for you? I'll get to that in minute before I clarify something...

You don't just "get" an agent: an agent agrees to sign you as a client.

Agents, for the most part, are just as exclusive and elitist as anyone else in the business, and it is hard to get through the door. Of course, the conventional wisdom is that agents should be salivating for clients -- and for the most part, they are eager to find new and promising talent.

However, when I am asked the question "Can you recommend an agent?" The simple answer is: I don't recommend THEM to you, I recommend YOU to them... and in doing so, I am putting my name behind the notion that the time they spent reading your writing samples for consideration will not be wasted. Because most agents already have vast lists of clients for whom they are actively trying to find work, their number one priority is making sure their time isn't wasted...

And frankly, I don't want their time wasted either (I

want them engaged in the task of finding me work!). For a long time, I did not send other people's writing samples to my agents. This flat across-the-board refusal often cost me in terms of personal capital and good will, but it did tend to be a lot easier than having to explain if I didn't think a person's writing was very good and I didn't feel comfortable putting my name behind it -- or if I just didn't have the time to read the material, or if I didn't think that person would be a good personality match for my agent.

The fact is, I get asked to read material almost daily. Sometimes it's by people I actually know, sometimes by people with extremely tangential connections to me, and most often from people who believe that having watched an episode or two that I wrote in the past gives them a claim on my time and energy.

When I don't just say no, I often wind up putting the actual reading off for so long that everyone's feelings are hurt and my best intentions wind up roadkill on the highway to hell. Of course, if I read all the material offered to me, gave notes and found an agent of my acquaintance willing to actually consider the material, I'd have no time to actually do my work, see my wife, pet the dogs and -- on occasion -- blog (which we all know to be the single most important activity on the earth).

So saying up front "I won't send you to my agent because I don't send anyone to my agent" often thins the herd a little -- especially from those who are just being mercenary and want me to get them an agent to those who may actually take my advice on how to improve their work. In the past few years, I have relaxed this policy a little -- JUST a little -- but only because I have gotten more comfortable telling people when I don't feel it is appropriate to submit their work, or, if in my opinion they are just not ready for primetime, or if I just don't have the time to read their stuff.

OK, I know the next question -- "How did YOU get your agents, smartypants?" Well, I took a shortcut... I wrote some 26 works for the stage by the time I got out of college, went to film school, got a Masters Degree in screenwriting, detoured into a two-year stint as a network executive and AFTER I had secured my first writing job, I called an agent with whom I had developed a friendship and asked him to represent me. It was a good deal for the agent -- worst case he got to commission ten percent of my first job and if I worked out, he had a proven client on his hands: and it worked very well. I have had the same representation for 11 years.

This touches on the number one emotional truth of the entertainment industry -- and the number one reason why agents are necessary. Rejection.

I know what you're thinking: "now wait just one minute there, ko-cheese, surely an agent's job is to navigate the maze-like structure of the industry -- to make hundreds of contacts among the executive hierarchies of studios, networks and all the other buyers of material and hirers of writers, to figure out the companies making the product most compatible with the writing/directing/acting style of their clients, and make sure they are a given a fair hearing, to negotiate deals and continually increase the income-earning potential of their clients -- not just to be brokers of rejection!"

And you'd be right. However -- in addition to all that, the most vital thing an agent does is to be the public face of the client -- and to provide a value-neutral venue for the rejection of that person's writing.

Consider this. You are an executive at a studio. Your

studio has 20 pilots in production. Only five of them will be ordered to series by a broadcast network. The average show has anywhere from five to nine writers on staff.

A total of 500 to 700 scripts have been sent to you by agents who want you to consider their clients for these twenty-five or so jobs -- and here's the clincher -- you don't actually decide who gets those jobs! Your job is actually to try to find people who might be good for the writing job and recommend them to the person who is actually running those shows.

Now what sounds like an easier task for you, theoretical executive?

Calling the agents who represent those writers and brushing it all off with a simple "I didn't respond to the material" (which is universal entertainment industry shorthand for any number of things from "I didn't like it" to "I was driving my car, playing Tetris and talking on the phone when I read it") which the agent will accept without muss or fuss (before trying to do an end run around you to get the material to the showrunner anyway)... or...

Having to personally speak to the writers of each of those scripts, explain why you didn't like their work, and, subsequently, console them during the inevitable "I'll-never-work-again-why-doesn't-anybody-LOVE-me?" meltdown?

Yeah, I thought so.

Long story short: consoling writers is not the job of a studio executive. Thanks to the agent-as-intermediary-of-rejection system, by the time the pass gets from the exec to the writer, it is usually delivered with such a businesslike matter-of-factness, earned in the course of a long-lived-in agent/writer relationship, that the devastating emotional punch is diluted from "I'll-never-work-again-why-doesn't-anybody-LOVE-me?" to a vague feeling of unease.

The truth is NO one wants to talk to the writer directly before the writer has been hired. NO one wants to tell another person that the piece of their soul they have just served up in 60 laser-printed pages is just not good enough... and this is why no one EVER just "submits" their work to a studio. The current system -- flawed, unfair, elitist and recondite though it may be -- is a harmony of intermediary perfection. It is designed to create the least amount of psychic pain possible... which, given the amount of psychic pain it inflicts as it is, is kind of a blessing.

Kind of.

So let's say you have spent the requisite amount of time honing your craft -- have made a decision about whether or not you want to be a drama or comedy writer (two vastly different disciplines requiring pretty diverse skill-sets) -- written several absolutely bulletproof writing samples that will leave even the most jaded reader with the impression that you are a major talent and cannot be denied, found someone through your travels -- someone with a connection to an agent who is not only willing to read your work (already an imposition) but also to cash in a favor to give it to an agent...

And let's say the agent actually reads it -- or that, more likely, the agent's assistant reads it and likes it enough to recommend it to the agent, who then reads it (and, depending on that agent's rank within the agency, may have to ask several other agents to read it and approve before they can take you on) -- schedules a meeting with you to make sure you are presentable, then signs you up as a client...

Employment is pretty much ensured, right?

Riiiiight.

PART TWO

L et's say you're a doctor... now dig, if you will, that the only way you could get a job... er... doctoring, was by being in one city for three months -- and competing with every other MD in the country during those three months.

That's what it's like to write for TV.

Currently, we are in the throes of what is known as "staffing season." Much has already been written about staffing season -- mostly by industry insiders with blogs -- so I'll try to keep it light and entertaining.

Staffing season takes place at the same time as "pilot season" -- the time of the year when the networks order and the studios produce pilot episodes for proposed new series. The culmination of all this is the "network Upfronts" -- a yearly presentation of all the networks' fall schedules to advertisers -- which take place in May. It is there that the networks drop their shrouds of secrecy after months of speculation and formally announce which pilots are going to become series and which are going to become war stories for embittered writers.

Staffing is essentially the concomitant all-city-TV-writer-job-fair. As the pilots come in and it becomes more and more clear which are going to series, those writers lucky enough to be making a pilot actively look for other writers who can execute their vision...

Meanwhile, those lucky enough to be running a show that is already on the air and will stay on are looking for new writers to replace all the ones that "didn't work out" over the year...

And those who are unemployed (or are in the process of "not working out" at whatever show employed them in the previous season) are tied to their phones, waiting for their agent to call...

Why?

Because -- as I explained in part one -- your agent is the one submitting your work to the various intermediaries who stand between you and a lucrative job as a television writer.

Classically, the pyramid goes a little something like this -- the agent submits your work to both the network and studio executives, whose job it is to be the liaison between the person writing/producing the pilot and the outside world, and uses all of their personal powers of persuasion to get them to read you...

Now, if the studio and network executives like you -- and if enough of them like you -- they start talking to the various showrunners they have creating television for them.

Then -- as if by magic, or mostly because they have heard your name spoken positively by so many people -- the showrunner may just decide to read your writing sample... and maybe even hire you.

But there is one more hurdle before you go meet the showrunner. Let's say that the studio and network executives -- and there are many at either establishment -- like your stuff. Good.

Before you get to meet the Great and Mighty Oz, the executives at both studio and network may call you in for a meeting. This is usually a "general meeting" -- in which they decide if you are presentable to any and all of the showrunners they have either making shows or pilots. By "presentable" I mean of sound mind and body -- speaks well, fluent in English, no drooling, no fulminant odors, un-lanced boils or weeping, exposed lacerations. They may also make some judgment as to whether or not you may be a good fit for the show personality-wise -- but not before they decide about the fulminant body odor.

If you pass these minimum requirements for presentability, the studio and/or network will speak on your behalf to the showrunner... who will then read you and, if they like what they see, call you in for a meeting.

Then comes the strange part. You go in to meet with a showrunner, and the next 30 minutes of your life will literally decide whether or not -- for the duration of the TV season -- you will be spending more time with, and trying to understand the mind of, this person and those she/he hires than anyone else in your life.

Because that's what it means to write for TV -- you will spend more time in direct emotional communion with the people in the writers room than with your spouse, children and/or pets. The sum and substance of your existence becomes the weird, mutant hybrid of dodgeball, group therapy, and the Bataan Death March that is working with up to nine other people on making a season of television... and this is usually decided in a meeting that will last anywhere from one-half to a full hour.

I have gone out for one job in corporate America -- with NBC in 1993. It took several months, three interviews and a number of written creative exercises for them to finally pull the trigger and make an offer. Most people who seek others for employment have the luxury of time: most industrial concerns will survive the weeks or months it takes to find a new employee, and go through whatever hoops they deem necessary to find the person they consider best suited for the job (doesn't always work out, but there it is)...

TV is much more seat-of-the-pants.

Of course, that's one reason why it's a good idea to take a long view and cultivate a good reputation -- to have good working relationships with people. Usually before or after that half-hour, the showrunner will look at your resume and call other showrunners you have worked for. You better make sure they will have good things to say.

It's also important to understand that, more likely than not -- in every job you get -- you will be stepping into a situation in which you don't know all the variables and the personalities may not fully reveal themselves to you until much later.

The reason for this is, of course, the time-sensitivity of it all. Network shows get picked up in May, start production in July, and they air in September. Once shooting begins, the beast that is production eats a new script every eight business days, and the enterprise can never shut down -- not only because missing an airdate is the one unpardonable sin of network television, but also because the 150-person crew it takes to make a television show has to be paid every day in order to keep them in place. There is no time to dawdle! THE SPICE MUST FLOW!

This also makes for some very volatile workplaces... and is a reason why so many shows have so much turnaround in terms of their staffs.

Staffing season is a mad dash to get the best writers at a time when they are all being read, interviewed, and hired. There isn't always the time to put together a "cast" that is entirely compatible. There are millions of tales of writing staffs that looked tremendously promising on paper only to implode precisely because the hiring decisions were made according to who looked best on paper as opposed to whether or not everyone would get along.

But the system is what it is and -- for the most part -- it works. It cannot really be judged by the standards of other businesses because, while the business has long-established protocols, every show is, essentially, a start-up -- a completely new business with an essentially untested product of which there has only been one prototype: the pilot episode. When the result of those weird 30 to 60 minute meetings is a staff that gels, the end product is a TV shows you watch and love.

A lot of people complain bitterly about the general insensitivity and awfulness of the entertainment industry. Frankly, I am not sure it's all that different from hundreds of other professions (including the clergy) in terms of the awful things people do to one another. I find that cruel people tend to find their way into all walks of life and just sit there, coiled, waiting for a venue and a victim. That much said, we certainly make for colorful satirical fodder.

Truthfully, I don't find a lot of downside to the work I do -- and I do not intend for what I am about to say to be taken in any way as a complaint -- but I have noticed that there is a relatively unique emotional dimension to this career...

As I mentioned before, when you walk into a writers' room, you are meeting people you will see 10 hours a day, every working day for the next nine months. You will get to know them inside out -- they will annoy, infuriate, and, on occasion, entertain you. You will get to know their lives, their complexities -- and, from the things they don't tell you (or don't slip out in the inevitable moments of weary honesty) -- you may just be able to intuit from how they organize the dramatic construction of their stories.

The result is that you wind up having extremely intense short-term relationships with a lot of individuals... and the one defining characteristic of those relationships is that they drift away once the show is over. It is rare to "stay in touch" -- try as you might, and as fond as you may be of the people with whom you have staffed -- because once that common bond of working together and cohesively on mission-critical projects is removed, so is the *raison d'être* for the relationship itself. People just have a habit of drifting back into the substance of their own lives once the "rolling crisis" mentality of a long TV season is removed.

It is, however, a weird thing when one of the rote conditions of your work is constant preparation for the inevitable rupture in relationships that have grown incredibly close, incredibly fast. In the past 11 years, I have worked on eight different shows -- and the longest I have stayed at any place is two seasons (on *Lost* and *Charmed* -- and, by the way, in any other business, that kind of resume is a serious red flag. In TV, it's called "a successful career").

If I were to meet anyone from any of those staffs today, I would invariably have hours worth of war stories and reminiscences... the camaraderie is there, the memories, but also the realization that had you not been thrown together into that room, you might not have become friends at all. There is also a major upside -- I am never bored and am constantly meeting new, stimulating people with incredible stories to tell.

Two of my fellow *Lost* writers gave a talk at their alma mater a few weeks back. Somewhat surprisingly, they were asked what the show would be like without me working there anymore. I suppose that there has been some awareness of my contribution to the series outside of the fan community, and some publicity surrounding my departure from the series -- something that is extremely rare in TV, where writers tend to never share the spotlight with the actors.

Flattered as I am that someone would think my contribution so visible as to make a distinct difference in the quality of the show -- the telling detail of the exchange was the answer, because it speaks volumes about something more important -- the dynamic of a good writers room. Touchingly, my former co-workers compared my departure from *Lost* to having a friend in high school who is a year older and graduates ahead of you.

When I think about that statement, I wonder if that is not the best analogy I can give someone who doesn't work in TV and wants to know what it's like...

Like I never stopped applying for college.

SO YOU WANT TO WRITE A TELEVISION PILOT?

Originally published December 12th, 2004, on Livejournal.

DISCLAIMER

Although I can neither renounce my biases nor curb the natural inclination to make myself more heroic than I was in the situations I recount, the following is intended as *reportage* -- not complaint.

Let me repeat that: I have the single best job in the world... I only complain about it to those who know me well enough to tell me to stop my damned whining already.

A good friend of mine uses as a mantra Hyman Roth's statement "This is the business that we have chosen," and that is especially true of working TV writers. Few people just "wind up" here. Folks like me write for television because we want to -- very badly. Contrary to popular belief, the option of cashing out and raising goats in Yucaipa is always available.

So if you ever hear me mewling like a wounded lamb while stewarding a multi-million-dollar network and studio investment in something I created ("The network doesn't respect my show!" "I'm not getting enough promotion!" "Why did they cancel my series when I worked so hard on it?"), feel free to slap me like a bitch.

No, seriously. The life of a working television writer -- the exposure, the opportunities, the fact that you write something and an army of talented people goes out and makes it -- is too good. Complaining to fans is just bad form.

For example -- as heartbroken as I was over the cancellation of *Jake 2.0*, it's just plain immature for a writer/producer to complain about the network "not supporting the show" when they picked it up for a back-nine episodes even though it fell below the ratings of the show that bombed in the time slot the previous season...

And a rerun of *America's Next Top Model* did twice its ratings in the time slot.

That much said, it is damn funny that the network called us the morning after that rerun of *America's Next Top Model* aired in our time slot, asked us what episode we were filming, and then said, "Yeah, so just finish that one and then... GET OUT!"

That's not complaining, that's reporting an amusing -- if cruel -- truth.

Because when it's all said and done (well, when it's all said and done, there is usually more said than done, but aside from that) a television writer has a single responsibility:

To create commercial success for a television network.

I do not believe that I am entitled to anything from my would-be corporate masters -- not love, not support, not the paternal affirmation I never received as a child -- aside from a fair paycheck for services rendered.

The dirty truth of selling a television series is this: all you really did was persuade a bank to give you a loan to build a temporary dwelling of your own design on land they already owned. Success -- artistic or financial -- merely extends the span of your tenancy.

That's how they interpret the contract. That's how you should as well.

That much said, if you are a fan of a series, any series -- I EXPECT you to complain if it gets unfairly cancelled, or if it deserved better than it got, or if it never got its due. That is an essential part of the fan lifestyle, and your part in the great equation. My privilege is to make television -- yours is to judge whether it's good or bad, and, most importantly, deserving of your loyalty.

SO ANYWAY... PILOTS

The one question I hear most nowadays is "I have a great idea for a pilot, what do I have to do to get it see/produced/on the air?"

The stock answer to this is "move to Los Angeles and spend 10 years making a name for yourself as a television producer with an established track record that will make a studio and network believe that they should trust you with 44 million dollars of their money to produce 22 hours of television."

However, things have changed in television, and now it is easier than ever to get a pilot on the air without establishing a track record as a producer...

And I say that in the same way one might say, "Now it's easier than ever to put an orbital mind-control laser in a geosynchronous orbit over your mother-in-law."

If you are a feature writer who has made a big sale, or gotten a film produced -- or if you are a big-time film producer or director -- television is wide open. Whether you know TV, like it, or want to make it, the networks and studios believe that well-known, successful writer/ producer/directors are a pre-sold brand and a good barometer of potential success -- and will offer huge bucks to attract that talent.

JJ Abrams, Joss Whedon, and Jerry Bruckheimer are perfect examples of people who have parlayed their success in feature films into television empires marked by innovation and quality...

And being as I am currently employed by one of them, I am grateful for that.

However, for every Abrams, Whedon or Bruckheimer -- people who genuinely love TV, don't look down on the medium, and truly want to make their shows good -- there are dozens of feature writers, directors, and producers who have tried to turn their fame into success in television and failed.

The other phenomenon that makes it easier to sell pilots without necessarily having a long-running television career is that of the "pod."

Bruckheimer, Bad Robot, and Mutant Enemy are considered pods -- mini studios within the studios in which established television producers are able to use their name and clout to find new talent, develop pilots -- and leverage their resources and experience into a guarantee that even if the pilot is being written by someone untested, the film that will come out the other end will be up to snuff.

Of course, becoming an established feature film talent, entering into a relationship with a pod, or becoming a known television producer with a trustworthy track record all assume that you are a part of the industry, have an agent and, most importantly, have a property that is attractive to the networks.

And that's the real rub -- Because having a property that is attractive to the networks hinges on one non-negotiable fact: you actually have to be able to write it. Well.

Ideas are a dime a dozen -- and chances are that if you, or I, or, really, anyone -- has a pilot idea, it has already been pitched and developed at least once in the history of television.

Consider the numbers: during the time I worked as a network executive, I probably heard some 200 television pitches for drama series, and I was the bottom head on the totem pole. I wasn't really getting the totality of the game.

But let's say, as an order-of-magnitude calculation, that there were exactly two-hundred pitches on my first season in development. The network paid for some thirty to become scripts. Of the 30, the network green-lit -- maybe -- six. Of the six, maybe three made the fall schedule.

Divide that times six television networks -- that's 1,800 ideas for television shows every single year. Of course, most of these pitches make the rounds to more than one network, so my figure is probably inflated -- but boy howdy is it impressive!

So, given the numbers, chances are that even the most out-there premise (a syphillitic nun and a time-traveling, genetically enhanced muskrat use advanced forensic technology to root out criminals during the Dark Ages!) has been, at some point, heard and purchased -- or rejected -- by network executives.

The way to sell a pitch is by coming in with a fresh take on the material, and being able to convince the network that you -- and you alone -- can execute that premise in a way that they have not seen before. So let's say you have a pilot idea -- something you truly need to see in television.

You can't write it as a novel or comic book, or a series of flash cartoons on the web, or make it as an independent film. You want it to be in television more than anything else...

Then come out to Los Angeles, get in the business and make your play.

It's not easy, but neither is writing a novel, making a film, or writing a comic book... and, as with novels, comic books, and independent films, it's absolutely possible to get there.

Just remember, you had better be in it for the long haul, you'd better have more than one good idea -- and you'd better believe in your talent, patience and ability almost to the point of delusion -- because, believe you me, they will be tested.

Tested? Yep. Tested. How?

Here are three case studies, from the mixed-up files of Mr. Javier Grillo-Marxuach, that illustrate some of the many pitfalls of trying to develop television shows. The situations have been heavily fictionalized on the advice of James Mandelbaum, esq. (my attorney) and all the names have been changed to protect the innocent... as well the guilty, the ones who ought to have known better, and the ones who just wandered into the crossfire and caught some shrapnel as a result.

CASE STUDY #1 -- *THE FRANKENSTEIN PAPERS*
My agent arranged for a meeting with the development executives of the Gregor Framkin company, a well-funded studio with a large investment in family programming and a small primetime television division interested in expanding their operations. The meeting went exceedingly well and the executives mentioned they wanted to develop

a modern-day version of the Frankenstein story -- Victor Frankenstein as a monster hunter in the world of today.

At the time, I was a grunt writer working my second job on a series -- but in my off time, I developed a pilot format and story based on the rich literary lore of the character...

An epic tale in which the last descendant of Victor Frankenstein learns of his awful family past when his great-great-grandfather's monster comes back to life for a final death match. I pitched it to the Gregor Framkin company executives and they were interested in moving ahead...

For a month and a half, we refined the pitch, then took it to the UBS network.

The executives at UBS loved it so much they bought it in the room -- seconds after I stopped talking. For a young, inexperienced writer, this was a splendid, triumphant day.

However, two weeks later, I received a call that UBS did not want me to use the pilot story I had developed over the past two months. Apparently, another network had begun production on a new series entitled *Taffy the Golem Hunter* -- and they worried that a pilot about Doctor Frankenstein fighting his monster would be considered "derivative."

In spite of my protest that Doctor Frankenstein's monster was technically NOT a golem -- and that the two series couldn't be tonally more different -- the objection stuck and I was faced with the task of developing a new pilot story out of whole cloth in less than two weeks...

And lest we forget, I had a day job at the time, and not a lot of professional experience. Coming up with a new pilot story that would establish an entire series -- in less than two weeks -- was a task for which I simply did not have the time creative resources... I was in way over my head.

So the good folk at the Gregor Framkin company (they truly wanted me to succeed and supported me way above and beyond the call of duty) working with my agent, found two seasoned writers who agreed to come in as Executive Producers on the project.

Together we developed a new story: years after having faced and destroyed his great-great-grandfather's creature, Doctor Frankenstein, having taken up the mantle of monster hunter, and conquered many a foe, now found himself on the trail of an unfrozen prehistoric gila monster in the employ of a corrupt, burned-out homicide detective, who is using the creature to ice criminals who have slipped through loopholes in the criminal justice system.

I wrote a first draft based on the story, the two consulting writers did a rewrite, the network greenlit the script -- allowing us to film the pilot -- and we started casting and interviewing potential directors. What could possibly go wrong?

Quite a bit, apparently.

It turns out that only a year before, the Federal Government -- in a final gasp of post-Reagan Era monopolistic fervor -- revoked the laws against networks owning the programming they aired. This used to be taboo, as it was thought that, without regulation, the networks would give their in-house production units an unfair advantage.

Doing exactly that which the laws were designed to prevent, UBS promptly demanded to be given 50 percent ownership of *The Frankenstein Papers*... or they would revoke their greenlight.

The Gregor Framkin Company had no choice but to

capitulate to what was, essentially, an act of corporate extortion. Otherwise, our hard work would have gone down the drain. UBS Studios, the wholly owned, in-house production subsidiary of the UBS network, became half-owner and production partner on *The Frankenstein Papers*.

Additionally, the President of UBS Studios simply did not think that a small outfit like the Gregor Framkin Company, nor the team they had put together -- myself and the two Executive Producers who helped me out when I could not come up with a new story for the pilot -- would truly be able to deliver a good show. Immediately, they insisted that new Executive Producers with an even more established track record be brought in to insure the quality of the pilot and potential series.

The Gregor Framkin Company tried to stand firm in their opposition, but the network supported their studio and two new Executive Producers (they worked as a team) were recruited to make sure the project got past the finish line. These two Executive Producers felt that the dialogue in the original pilot script was too "arch and gothic" -- so they brought in one of their own favorite writers to make some changes.

And let me tell you: the words spoken during the hunt for a giant gila monster have NEVER sounded so gritty and grounded and true as they did in the shooting script of *The Frankenstein Papers*.

For those of you counting at home: without shooting a single frame, the project now had two studios, five Executive Producers (Gregor Framkin himself, who automatically takes a credit on all the shows produced by his company, the two writers who worked with me on the pilot, and the two Executive Producers brought in by UBS) -- one Supervising Producer (that's me, too young and inexperienced to receive an Executive Producer credit), three French hens, two turtle doves, and a partridge in a pear tree.

The pilot was ultimately cast and filmed... with much *sturm-und-drang* between the Gregor Framkin company and UBS Studios, a noisy walkout by the two Executive Producers who co-wrote the original draft with me, and vague sense of unease and general animosity between everyone else.

Somehow, by being young, inexperienced and eager to learn, I actually managed to stick around, become friends with most of the parties involved, learn to appreciate their talents and contributions, watch my first pilot get filmed, and even have a fair amount of input into the process...

And believe it or not, the final film wasn't all that bad...

But it was rejected by the UBS network...

The reason?

The actor cast in the role of Doctor Frankenstein looked "too young."

Instead, UBS premiered a competing sci-fi series entitled *Night Freaks* -- a dark, moody, *X-Files*-like supernatural procedural about insomniacs who solved crimes but got frequent headaches and couldn't think straight. *Night Freaks* was cancelled after its second airing.

Lesson learned: I got in way over my head. I had neither the resources to roll with the punches and make course adjustments, nor the juice to say, "It's my way or the freeway." I just wasn't "The Guy."

In this case, a lot of talented high-level people got involved in the project -- all of them trying to be "The Guy" and, as a result, whose creative vision became more and more diffuse with each new participant. Though the project limped to completion with a modicum of creative dignity, this would have been a nightmare of a series: several parties vying for creative control, multiple Executive Producers, and no one person responsible for the unifying vision.

It would have been unlikely that -- even as a series creator -- I would have been able to in any way influence the creative process toward something I would have been proud to have my name attached to. More likely than not, I would have either left the series, or been fired, at the end of the first season.

CASE STUDY #2 -- *THE ASSKICKER!*

I was toiling away on *The Hepcats* -- a doomed series about a team of Vespa-riding messengers hired by a top secret government agency to use their highly acrobatic scooter skills to take out the criminals the Feds JUST couldn't nail -- when I got a call from a friend at the UBS network...

Apparently UBS had just signed a contract with an up-and-coming young actor fresh out of one of their daytime soap operas -- let's call him "Armando Peludo."

Armando Peludo had the kind of charisma that makes women swoon and men want to shake his hand. Total *Mutual-of-Omaha's-Wild-Kingdom*-animal-magnetism combined with incredible acting chops.

Armando also had a very unique look -- over six feet tall, beautiful dark skin, intense cobalt-blue eyes and long, curly hair. A physical presence this unique would pretty much be wasted in something as mundane as a cop show.

Did I have an idea for a single-lead show for a slightly off-center actor?

Why, yes I did -- and it was called... *The Asskicker!*

An Aztec warrior, brought to the twentieth century (yes, Mr. Peabody, set the Wayback machine to that long-ago time known as "the late '90s") by mysterious forces and blessed with the ability to speak English, *The Asskicker!* now roams the streets and highways of America... using unique Mesoamerican martial arts to take down the bad guys in the name of Quetzalcoatl -- winged deity of pre-Columbian justice!

UBS hated it. They thought it was "too sci-fi."

My agent liked it, however, and suggested that we take it to the Big Time Network (BTN) -- a young, upstart channel with a taste for more "out there" programming.

BTN loved *The Asskicker!* They bought it in the room (lesson learned: I talked a good game, but did I have the chops to back it up in script?) -- where they also approved both the series concept and the pilot story. The game was afoot...

But BTN didn't think I was a veteran enough producer to deliver a good pilot (seeing the pattern?). They suggested that we (and by "we" they meant me) recruit a successful guy with a major track record -- let's call him "Producer A." He happened to be one of BTN's favorite people -- with whom they claimed to have a long-standing relationship.

Which made me wonder: if they had a long-standing relationship with the guy, why did they send me off to make the contact instead of calling him up themselves? That should have made red flags go up immediately...

But more on that in a minute.

Anyway, I dutifully arranged a meeting with Producer A, and sent him the script in advance. Yes, the script.

See, in my free time, I actually wrote the script to prove to myself that the story for *The Asskicker!* actually worked. I didn't show it to the brass at BTN, but it made the pitch easier to sell because I wasn't speaking theoretically. I had answers to all their questions because I knew the subject matter in and out.

By the way -- about this meeting I arranged -- well, I contacted Producer A, not through my agent, but through a friend who happened to be Producer A's assistant.

Big mistake -- why?

Because from the beginning, Producer A saw me not as a peer, but as his assistant's "little buddy" who lucked into selling a pilot and needed his help.

Lesson learned: don't ever make a call you can have your "people" make for you.

Also, never let anybody call you "buddy," if you aren't willing to let them see you as an inferior.

Anyway, Producer A read *The Asskicker!* and loved... the premise.

Yep, the premise... and only the premise.

But he still wanted to get involved. Why? It turned out that Producer A's first writing gig ever was the short-lived cult hit *Nightboar of New York* -- the darkly romantic tale of a young policewoman's impossible love for a noble, crime-fighting anthropomorphic man-pig who lived in a cave in Central Park (it still shows up on cable every once in a while). For a long time, Producer A had truly yearned to do something in a similar vein.

Before continuing, let's revisit the issue of why BTN didn't call Producer A on my behalf. At the time, Producer A was under contract to do a show for another network... but he liked the premise of *The Asskicker!* so much that he decided to get involved.

BTN didn't want to make the call themselves because they would be poaching on another network's contract -- by sending me in, a little guy who lucked into selling a pilot, they had plausible deniability. Not to mention that what I did by getting him "pregnant" with *The Asskicker!* meant that he would go the extra mile to smooth things over with his other corporate overlords who would balk at the idea of him doing a show for a rival network.

Lesson learned: don't be anyone's monkey. If some big organization isn't willing to make the call on your behalf, don't make the call for them -- ask them why.

Did I mention that *The Asskicker!* was sold very late in the development season?

That's an important detail: because we sold *The Asskicker!* in October, when most networks have already closed up shop -- having bought their pilot pitches between July and September -- I had to execute Producer A's page one rewrite in about a week and a half in order to get the script in to the network brass in time to decide whether or not to greenlight the thing.

So I moved into the office next door to Producer A. While he worked on his other show -- and before anybody could protest, but also before a formal deal could be made -- we created a new story and I wrote nonstop.

While still called *The Asskicker!,* the new script was a lot softer now and featured considerably less kicking of ass than promised by the title. Heavily influenced by the urban-gothic-fantasy tone of *Nightboar of New York*, this version of *The Asskicker!* was a dark, brooding romance in which The Asskicker voluntarily transported himself from pre-Columbian Mexico to modern day Los Angeles to protect a beautiful, crusading Chicano lawyer who may or may not have been the reincarnation of his dead Aztec Princess wife.

In the meantime, the other network with whom Producer A had a contract got massively pissed off that their man was working on a series for another network and came to think of me as the antichrist for diverting Producer A's focus. To this day, I have not worked on a show for that network.

Now, during the rewriting process, the Vice President in charge of Drama Development at BTN was told -- very specifically -- by both me and Producer A, about the changes being made to *The Asskicker!*

However, on the day the script was turned in two things happened...

Producer A went out of the country on vacation and I received a very peevish call from the VP: where the hell was the show I sold them, the show they bought in the room? I pitched an edgy action/adventure about an ass-kicking Aztec warrior and delivered a brooding romance about a Chicano lawyer!

So, being the go-get-them guy that I am, I decided that if Producer A chose to leave the country at this crucial moment, the responsibility was on me to save the project... and I told the VP that I had already written the script for the series I pitched.

Naturally, he asked to read it... and the next day, I got an ecstatic call. He loved it!

His next question? Why didn't I give them this script in the first place? (uh...because they were so hell bent on getting Producer A involved at that time that it wouldn't have mattered!)

Then came the kicker... would it be OK if I did script revisions on both my version and the one I wrote with Producer A? You know, since we'd come this far, why not have two scripts to choose from?

I got no sleep for the next three days. I was like a cast member from that short-lived series *Night Freaks*. I did all their notes and rewrites -- and, for a moment, I was in the weird position of having written competing projects, both named *The Asskicker!*, and both at the same network.

The word finally came in a week later. I won the lottery! The network wanted to greenlight *The Asskicker!*

My version. <u>The show I sold them</u>.

Producer A -- who, in spite of everything, truly had done me a big favor by getting involved -- and I parted ways amicably and remain friends to this day -- but I was right back where I started: an untested writer / producer who, in spite of having written the script the network wanted to produce, was not trusted to head the production, manage a multi-million dollar budget, hire a director and deliver a great pilot.

BTN, and Big Time Studios (BTS), the network's corporate partner was handed the project for production... and they went on the hunt for a showrunner.

Ultimately, they settled on Producer Z.

Being a Huge Deal, Producer Z would not deign to sit down with me and talk about the project until his deal to Executive Produce the pilot and series was complete. However, during that time, I met with the BTS brass and they assured me that just because they were going to pay a guy a huge amount of money to come in and Executive Produce my pilot and showrun a potential series didn't mean it wouldn't be my project anymore.

At most -- I was told -- Producer Z would do a "dialogue polish" to show that he was involved, and I would still be able to see my creative vision on the screen and be actively involved in the running of the series.

Several days passed after that meeting. Producer Z's deal finally closed, and he called to tell me that we needed to "swap some spit." Rather than to tell him that his metaphor was not entirely correct and more than a little inappropriate -- I rushed over to his office to talk to him.

Actually, I didn't rush to his office. I went and bought a new shirt and had my car washed. Why? Because I expected us to get along famously... and after talking for hours, we would go to lunch together, and at that lunch, we would see all sorts of famous celebrities, and brag to them about how I wrote a great script and he was just the man to bring it to the screen in all its glory.

Seriously, I was like Dirk Bogarde in the lead-up to the closing scene of Visconti's adaptation of *Death in Venice*... only in a bowling shirt and a Kangol beanie.

Fuck you, it was the '90s.

Upon arriving at his office to meet me, Producer Z's opening was to tell me that, for the past four days, he had been working closely with BTS on his complete and total rewrite of my pilot.

You heard that right. For. Four. Days.

Producer Z and the very same people who -- less than 12 hours before -- told me to my face that my creative vision would be respected had been completely revamping my pilot in their image long before his deal had closed.

After a few further awkward words, Producer Z excused himself because, he "had to get to the gym."

I called my agent. He screamed. I screamed. Everybody screamed... and before the dust settled, a messenger from the production office of my own pilot (an office I didn't even know existed, and to which I had never been invited -- much less offered a space) showed up on my doorstep with a script.

The cover read:

THE HISPANIC ANGEL OF BOYLE HEIGHTS
Written by Producer Z

Not only was my name nowhere to be seen, but the script told the heartbreaking, magical-realist story of a young Chicano cop, killed in the line of duty during the Watts riots and mysteriously brought back to life 30 years later to protect a single mother and an alcoholic priest trying to keep their neighborhood safe from gangs. This "Hispanic Angel of Boyle Heights" also played the saxophone on the roof of his tenement at night. You know, because he was a sensitive, artistic kinda guy.

Not unsurprisingly, the network got this script and screamed "where's the project we bought?!?" Big Time Studios -- which, along with Big Time Network was a wholly owned subsidiary of Big Time Global, and with whom they should have arguably had that mythical simpatico known as "corporate synergy" -- claimed that the network had agreed on Producer Z, and surely must have understood that "you don't get Producer Z without letting Producer Z do what Producer Z does. "

Although that's the price you apparently pay when you get Producer Z, BTN nonetheless insisted that Producer Z go back to my original version of the script.

You know, the show they bought.

In a spectacularly misplaced display of integrity, Producer Z held his ground, insisting that he would only produce his version of the show. Throwing their arms up in the air, the network pulled the greenlight and called it a day.

Lessons learned: trust no one. Believe no one. They'll suck your soul and then complain about how awful it tastes! The world wants you dead! Dead! Dead!

Uh. Sorry. Unresolved. Moving on.

After the debacle that was *The Asskicker!* I went

through a long period of mourning. I wondered why anyone would subject a potential collaborator and ally, someone coming to them in good faith with a golden egg -- a greenlit pilot at a network -- to so humiliating a level of betrayal.

There are two answers to this.

One is that BTS had spent a long time developing their own projects for BTN -- some of them even in the action/ adventure/supernatural arena -- and they didn't want a project they did not have their fingers in to succeed. It would have made them look bad.

The second explanation is simple. Have you ever wondered why big kids beat up smaller kids and take their milk money? Because they can.

CASE STUDY #3 -- *LUNAR JUSTICE*

After taking a very long break from developing television pilots in order to get some much-needed experience and establish a track record, I was approached by the GNX network. While techno-procedural cop shows like *CSI* and *NCIS* had become all the rage in the early days of the twenty-first century, a lot of executives were concerned about how to inject new life into the formula... did I have an idea?

Yes. I did.

Lunar Justice was a gritty, procedural cop drama set on Earth's first colony on the Moon. *Law & Order* set a hundred years from now... in SPACE! and dealing with the problems of future crimefighting in a realistic way that everyone -- not just sci-fi fans -- would be able to understand.

So I wrote the script, and it was good. The nice folk over at GNX loved it.

Also, I was now a trained, seasoned, professional producer with multiple seasons on various shows under my belt. In fact, one of the conditions of my contract was that I would be named Executive Producer of the pilot and officially anointed as "The Guy."

The problem with being anointed "The Guy," I would soon find out, is that no one can anoint you "The Guy." You're either "The Guy" or you're not. If you ever have to stop to think about whether or not you are "The Guy," you're not "The Guy."

Even with me on board as "The Guy," *Lunar Justice* was an expensive show. Also, a lot of people couldn't really visualize it. Just what does a futuristic procedural cop show look like? *Lunar Justice* also needed a large cast and a huge amount of special effects to convincingly render its out-of-this-world setting. GNX wasn't sure that their in-house production unit and wholly owned subsidiary, GNXS, had the resources to plunk down the above-average budget it would require to truly deliver on the promise of the script.

They did, however, like it enough to make a deal with me. They would keep the project on their development roster for a year, and during that year, they would pay me to write an additional two scripts for *Lunar Justice* to prove that there was indeed a viable series in the concept.

I took the deal, assuming that the project would most likely die on the vine. It's unusual for a project, no matter how well-liked, to survive for too long on a development slate before it gets stale -- before the executives move on to other things...

But then something amazing happened. During that interim year, Academy Award-winning director Richard Weinstock released his sci-fi opus *Moon Patrol*

-- an adaptation of the popular 1980s coin-op game. Weinstock's film was not only very good, it also raked in MONDO box-office.

Suddenly, there was a futuristic moon-based law enforcement gold rush! The biggest names in television were pitching moon-based procedural law-enforcement series!

Thankfully, GNX felt that they already had a winner with *Lunar Justice*, and to their credit, stuck with my project as their sole entry in the race. When the time came to grant the money to produce the series, however, the issue of the huge production costs for *Lunar Justice* came up with a vengeance.

A year had simply not changed the truth that GNXS simply did not have the money to make *Lunar Justice* and still produce the other pilots they needed to fill the other gaps in their schedule. *Lunar Justice* was an expensive gamble, and they just didn't have the chips.

But there was one way to get *Lunar Justice* made...

That same year, GNX struck a deal with multi-billion dollar movie producer Jimmy Gottrox. You've seen Mr. Gottrox's productions -- they are the kinds of movies that gross hundreds of millions of dollars, spawn countless sequels and make stars out of mere actors.

Gottrox is probably best known for his recent series of sci-fi epics entitled *The War of the Frodis:* a stand-up-and-cheer saga about the fight between men and intelligent plants for ultimate control of the planet. *The War of the Frodis* began as a standalone movie but promptly metastasized into a trilogy the moment the box-office grosses crossed the quarter-billion mark.

Later, the trilogy became a quadrilogy when the third film *The War of the Frodis 3: Rise of The Fallen Frodis*, split into *The War of the Frodis 3: Rise of The Fallen Frodis, Part One - Uprising,* and *The War of the Frodis 3: Rise of The Fallen Frodis, Part Two - Twilight of the Frodis...* presumably to give all the mammals at the watering hole their go at the carcass.

Through his company, Gottrox Entertainment -- a pod working as a subsidiary of my old friends from *The Asskicker!,* Big Time Studios -- Jimmy Gottrox was salivating to get into the hour-long drama business... but not out of a love of television.

Mostly, Jimmy Gottrox felt a deeply rooted resentment and envy for other feature film producers who managed to build television empires. Gottrox believed -- with an almost Jihadist fervor -- that if his rivals had footholds in television, then the industry <u>owed</u> him parity. His slogan -- oft repeated in a desperate, blustering howl -- was "I just want to WIN."

Gottrox's lucrative deal with GNX stipulated that his company would develop nine scripts. GNX was contractually bound to greenlight at least one of these scripts or pay a five-million-dollar penalty.

When all the scripts were turned in, it became very clear that Gottrox and his team had a sizable learning curve ahead of them before they'd have the capacity to develop a viable television format. More bluntly, GNX didn't want to produce any one of their shitty scripts... but they also didn't want to pay the exorbitant penalty or lose the opportunity to advertise a television series as being "from Jimmy Gottrox -- producer of *The Frodis Trilogy -- ahem -- Quadrilogy.*"

So GNX offered me a deal. Make *Lunar Justice* with Big Time Studios -- the same people who dealt me <u>so</u> a square deal on *The Asskicker!* -- under the aegis of Gottrox

Entertainment... or don't make *Lunar Justice* at all.

I loved *Lunar Justice*. Loved it with the kind of blinding passion that makes a person commit to idiotic decisions... the kind of passion it takes to commit to a career in television.

I took the deal -- and regretted it immediately.

In addition to his pictures, Jimmy Gottrox was known for two things: an extravagant lifestyle, and a management style that made Lavrenty "Beria" Pavlovich look like Oprah Winfrey.

Indeed, my first meeting with the man was -- to borrow a phrase from *The Birdhouse* -- like riding a psychotic horse into a burning barn. Or meeting Jabba the Hutt while standing on the Rancor pit trapdoor without a thermal detonator or Jedi powers to back me up.

From jump street, I realized I had made a grave error in judgment. I committed my beloved infant -- whom I had lovingly nurtured for the past year -- to the care of a predatory autocrat who not only appeared to have a breathtaking case of attention deficit hyperactivity disorder, but -- as far as I could tell -- had not even bothered to read the actual script for *Lunar Justice* (to this day I believe he never did)... and who would never in a million years actually allow me to produce the series as my own.

From that first meeting with Jimmy Gottrox, I realized that, although I was contractually named Executive Producer and had been anointed "The Guy," Jimmy Gottrox's overwhelming wealth and power -- and the truth that he held the strings on a billion-dollar feature franchise for BTS -- insured that if I were to ever disagree with him, I wouldn't just lose. I would also be severely punished for my insolence.

That basic inequality was obvious to me from the beginning... but like I said, I wanted to make *Lunar Justice* more than anything in the world... even though everything I saw was shouting "ALL ABOARD!" on the no-dinner-no-kiss-no-lube express train to fuck city.

Truly, the worst part of it is that *I knew it*. From that first meeting. From the moment I laid eyes on the guy. From the moment Jimmy Gottrox told me that there was only one place to film *Lunar Justice*:

The lush, tropical rain forests of Brazil.

Apparently, Gottrox had just spent over half a billion dollars filming episodes two and three of the *War of the Frodis* trilogy... er, quadrilogy... on the Amazon basin. He was convinced that he could deliver the epic look and feel of the *War of the Frodis* movies on a weekly television budget (about two million dollars per episode) if allowed to film there.

In his infinite largesse, Gottrox even suggested that if the series got picked up, I would move to the rain forests to supervise the whole thing while he stayed in the States and enjoyed his vast home, chauffeur, and the army of private chefs, and hot and cold running hookers kept on call to cater to his increasingly Orson Wellesian tastes.

I delicately made several counter-arguments. First, there is a massive difference between a five-hundred-million-dollar feature made on location after several years worth of intense logistical planning -- and a shooting schedule of over a year -- and a succession of two-million-dollar television series episodes each shot in the space of eight business days.

Second, American actors may not want to uproot themselves and their families to the tropical rain forests of Brazil for several years to work on a television show -- and that would affect their willingness to participate on the pilot.

Third, we were bound to have trouble convincing directors, writer/producers and guest cast to make a TV series in another country -- not only was Brazil not known as a hub for American television production, the rigors of relocation (especially for those married with children), language barrier, and tax issues, make these arrangements very tricky for the kind of talent one usually needs to pull off a pilot.

And fourth -- and I felt I this one was pretty unanswerable -- the tropical rain forests of Brazil could not possibly be made to pass for the surface of the moon!

When my -- rather practical, I thought -- concerns were ignored, I did something I promised myself I would never do. Something I always thought was a cowardly act.

I threatened to quit.

After I delivered my ultimatum, I was met by the very same BTS executive who, just a few years earlier, promised me that my creative vision for *The Asskicker!* would be respected. He told me not to worry: *Lunar Justice* would be my show, and the studio would protect me from Mr. Gottrox's worst impulses...

And son of a biscuit -- I don't know why -- but I bit into that manure sandwich like it was the most luscious sliver of punkin pie ever served.

Lesson learned: when someone offers you "protection," not only can they not provide it, they never intend to. They probably don't have the power to do so, but are merely saying it to make themselves feel important and put you in their debt.

Lesson #2: once you commit, quitting is not really an option. It makes everyone else look bad -- and that affects

your future employability. A good friend of mine put it
best when he told me that "The studios will do business
with someone who is difficult, but not with a terrorist."
When you walk off a high-budget, high-profile project
-- one that you originated, no less -- you tarnish the
enterprise; you broadcast to the entire business that the
project is in trouble.

And that is the most useless kind of power a person
can have. Like a neutron bomb, you can only use it once.
To take your ball and go home means you label yourself
as a volatile, difficult person who tanks projects. Of
course, to stay means to watch the protracted murder
by asphyxiation of your children... but at this point your
choices are limited.

In spite of the gamest and most courageous efforts of
a talented Brasilo-American cast and crew -- and in spite
of the incredible generosity and friendship I found as an
American television producer working abroad -- *Lunar
Justice* simply didn't work on film. Our four-and-a-half-
million-dollar pilot budget was just not enough to make
the tropical rain forests of Brazil look like the surface of the
moon.

There was, however, something vaguely endearing
about our efforts to make Brazil look like the moon...
the sort of thing that charitable souls refer to as "noble
failure."

Unfortunately, once we returned from Brazil -- the
arduous spade-and-trowel work of production complete
-- Jimmy Gottrox decided to re-assert his power over the
project by bringing his experience in "rescuing troubled
projects in the editing room" to bear on *Lunar Justice*.

Feeling that the material didn't "swing," Gottrox
personally sat in a throne-like leather recliner in the Avid

bay for several days -- precariously surviving only on restaurant food delivered by the one of his four assistants who was ever allowed to be away from the office phone -- personally instructing his editor on how to cut out every moment in the film that didn't "swing."

By the time Gottrox was done with his cut of the *Lunar Justice* pilot, a story that originally occupied the standard 43 minute running time of an American "hour" of television (remember, TV networks make money by selling commercial time within their shows) had been reduced to 21.5 swingin' minutes of pure entertainment... as re-assembled by someone whose editorial direction only added to my growing suspicion that he had never bothered to read the pilot script.

Making matters worse, Gottrox became incensed by my attachment to such things as plot cohesion, character motivation, and world-building exposition. These things, as he continually explained to me with endlessly escalating volume, didn't "swing." On the final day of editing before our first round of studio-funded audience testing -- an important step taken before the pilot is "locked" and shown to the network for series consideration -- I was greeted at the door to the editing suite by one of his lackeys, who let it be known that I was no longer "invited to take part in the post-production process."

Not unsurprisingly, test audiences who were shown Gottrox's "rescued" cut of *Lunar Justice* were "confused" as to the exact plot, characters, and narrative intentions. Also, the overwhelming majority never really got it from the viewing experience that the show took place on the moon.

Do you remember that moment in *Ferris Bueller's Day Off* when Ferris gives the "not by him" monologue to Cameron? That memorable scene in the Abe-Fromansausage-king-of-Chicago restaurant in which Ferris unpacks that, yes, someday someone is going to bust him: but it's not going to be "that guy" -- remember that?

That scene -- even though it takes place in a film I consider a hateful Valentine to rich white kid entitlement -- kept playing over and over in my head. Someday, someone is going to take everything away from me -- but I would be damned if I allowed it to be that cheap-souled, and possibly illiterate, vulgarian.

So I detonated The Nuclear Option.

I called the network directly. Disrupting the delicate do-si-do of "everything's-going-GREAT-we-promise" that goes on between networks and their suppliers before the former is given a chance to look at the product by the latter, I tattled to them about the cuts to the body of the pilot, the disastrous audience testing, and depredations I was suffering. I was a brave whistle-blower, alerting them to the Clear and Present Danger to the product they had purchased.

In a sequence of events worthy of Ferris Bueller himself, I cashed in every favor that was ever owed to me from my days at the network. I burned through my personal and professional capital with an abandon usually reserved for one-hit wonder musical acts at Aston Martin showrooms.

In the end, I marshaled the collective power of three network vice presidents, and together, we formed a phalanx that battering-rammed its way into that editing room. Thus armed -- and in the name of creative integrity -- we TOTALLY forced that vile film gangster to put back in the parts of the film that... uh, you know... explained the premise of the pilot.

I think you know how this story ends...

Even with all of the parts that explained the plot, characters and story, *Lunar Justice* was summarily rejected by GNX upon first viewing. No notes. No re-edit. No nothing. We got tapped out. Told to return our bat and glove -- and not even asked to hit the showers.

Lunar Justice was a serious disaster.

Strangely, as soon as the shit hit the fan, Jimmy Gottrox suddenly realized that the publicity for the launch of *The War of The Frodis 2 - Regeneration of the Frodis* needed the kind of help only he could provide... and so did post-production on the two-part-third-part-finale of the increasingly mislabeled trilogy. Apparently word got to him that it didn't "swing."

With a wave of his money and power, Jimmy Gottrox made himself very scarce from the debacle. His work of having made all but certain that a situation existed in which an already tenuous pilot was reduced from noble failure to unwatchable mess was complete.

Until very recently, my name was a killing word at BTS.

My friend was right: they won't do business with a terrorist. It's not like they need to blackball you: it's just that there are so many of us writers in the business. Why take another chance on someone who couldn't find a way to "make it work" with a major producer in whose success they were deeply invested?

BTS had not developed *Lunar Justice* -- it had been handed to them -- and that made it a red-haired step child from the get-go; not to mention that any potential success of it as a series was a theoretical compared to the very concrete profits to be made from *The War of the Frodis* This was the hardest blow. The one that hurt the most.

My job had not been to create, to produce or to write. My job -- and I suppose it was believed that I understood this implicitly -- was to build a Potemkin village to keep alive Jimmy Gottrox's illusions of beating JJ Abrams and Joss Whedon and Jerry Bruckheimer while the *Frodis* films generated the kind of profits that make the budgets of television pilots look like sandwich money.

It had been over before it began. All the battles had been less than meaningless: an annoyance to those who had been in on the joke all along.

Because God is Love, I did manage to escape largely unscathed in the eyes of the network -- who tend to view their financial investment in a TV pilot as more than sandwich money. I had, after all, created a show they truly wanted, delivered three high-quality scripts for the series, and had been so overruled by Jimmy Gottrox that there was little I could ultimately have done to ensure the quality of the product.

Lesson learned: in the real world, Ferris Bueller gets shot in the head by Homeland Security for attempting to hijack a parade float.

EPILOGUE -- DOES IT GET BETTER?

I will never stop trying to develop a television series that gets on the air. It's like scratching an itch. It's what I was made to do. The catastrophes I just recounted all came and went, and I am still here, a little wiser for the wear, and still more than willing to throw myself into the fray should the right idea come to pass...

However...

A long time ago, I came to the realization that a script is more than just "a blueprint to a film." To truly be a successful manifestation of the form, a script needs to be a work of art in and of itself. It requires the same strict integrity of a poem or novel.

A great script demands formal and structural elegance. It's not enough to have a great story and great dialogue: a great script is one that, at every level -- from the names of the characters to the layout of the words on the page -- creates an irresistible narrative flow that propels the reader to an inevitable dramatic conclusion.

This is the ideal for which I strive. Every day, I try to write scripts that will allow me to wake up the next morning -- no matter how badly a showrunner may butcher my work in rewrites, or how little of my original intent a director may ultimately deliver in the film, or how mercilessly an ill-prepared actor slaughters the lines -- and know that I did my job. All I want is to know, day in and out while on the job, that I created something worthy of professional pride.

Somewhere, in a hard drive, or on a shelf in my storage area, there are copies of three scripts that were supposed to become hit series... *The Frankenstein Papers, The Asskicker!* and *Lunar Justice*. They are good scripts -- and I like revisiting them. It's like looking at family pictures, reflecting my growth as a writer and how far I have come in my efforts to master the form since they were written.

And I do take comfort in knowing that these scripts were all good enough to be selected for production by the heads of major television networks... and they were also good enough to motivate otherwise rational people to act in the most irrational, immoral, deceitful, underhanded, and, occasionally, downright evil, ways to get a piece of the action...

And there are times when I think to myself that -- short of actually getting a series on the air -- that may be the best compliment a writer can get.

MAN OF PLANS, MAN OF IMPROV

Originally published March 26, 2006, on Livejournal.

I recently taught a writing workshop in my adopted home town of Ann Arbor, Michigan. Whenever I speak publicly, I am invariably asked the question "what television shows do you watch?"

For the past two years, the answer has always been the same. *24*, *Gilmore Girls*, and *Battlestar Galactica*. I have waxed rhapsodic about all three of these shows in the past, and won't reiterate here.

What was interesting about this version of the question was the follow-up -- how does it make me feel to know that *Galactica* series showrunner and mastermind Ronald D. Moore not only didn't have a plan for several of the story arcs of his series when the series began -- but also admits to it freely?

The question is germane to my work on *Lost* because so much has been made of "the plan."

It seems that much of the trust that audiences put on us as storytellers is based on the perception that only by knowing exactly where we are going can we tell the story we need to tell with the assurance that it will go somewhere great. In the case of *Lost*, it seems that the worst epithet people can throw at us nowadays is "they're just making it up."

There's a weird kind of hagiography that nowadays

forms around highly serialized shows and movies. It seems to be a point of pride -- and a great publicity angle -- to say, "I had this all figured out, I wrote it all out in a Big Chief notebook years before I sold the show, and everything is going exactly as I planned."

In some cases it's true. By many reputable accounts J. Michael Straczynski did -- indeed -- have a five-year plan for *Babylon 5*. Now, I personally think there was a fair bit of fancy footwork and improvisation involved to make that plan jump all the flaming hoops through which five seasons of television puts a show -- to which True Believers always counter the idea that the Great Maker cleverly laid trapdoors for himself -- providing detours for all narrative eventualities. To me, that just begs the question of where he found the time to actually make his show.

In other cases, the claim that everything was concretely laid out in advance is accurate only in the most generously accommodating sense possible. A study of the available drafts and outlines and early proposals for *Star Wars* and its sequels, prequels, and equals, makes it patently clear that while George Lucas may have had the broad strokes for what eventually became his sextet of films, his early explorations certainly did not make up a comprehensive plan for a story told over six movies. Or nine. It depends on which interview you read and when it was granted.

In the case of *Lost* the answer is pretty simple -- and has been reiterated by Damon Lindelof and Carlton Cuse in interview after interview. A bunch of writers -- myself, Paul Dini, Jennifer Johnson, and Christian Taylor -- were hired before the pilot was done and put together a lot of the conceptual framework of the show you see today.

From that work and everything the show's subsequent writing staff have built on it since, we figure out the road map and once we have front-loaded the series and the season with enough content that we are confident of the signposts illuminating the road ahead, the day-to-day work of the writing staff is putting those turns, twists and revelations into the dramatic events of a series of episodes. It is a system that allows us to be flexible and explore the things we find along the way while telling the tale we came to tell.

Because I am a fan of *Galactica* and not an active participant in its development, my answer to the question of how I feel about Ron Moore's admission to not having a plan was simple...

I don't care whether they have a plan, no plan, or a fragment of a plan because I trust Ron Moore. Now, I don't know Ron Moore save for meeting him socially over the years, but I do know his writing very well. I have been watching episodes written by the man since I was in college and he was selling freelance scripts to *Star Trek: The Next Generation* -- and I certainly know his reputation. I know from everything I have seen that this is not someone who takes on a property and blithely ignores such things as character and continuity.

Frankly, 10 times out of 10, I'm going to judge a show on my impression of its creators, and the writing and execution of their previous work over a belief -- or the creators' self-serving insistence -- that they have a plan. In some cases, I'm more interested in seeing someone I consider to be gifted improvising and flying by the seat of his/her pants than someone who can draw a map to microscopic detail.

Galactica is a fine example of that -- and frankly, one that is easier for me to discuss than *Lost* because I view *Lost* with the eyes of someone who has lived on the island for two years and for whom objectivity is a difficult thing.

The lesson all writers can learn from *Galactica*, however, is very similar from what I feel I have learned on *Lost*. Risk may just be the only thing left for television writers to explore in the 500-channel universe: a television environment in which every series idea ever conceived has probably been shot and put on the air at least once.

There was a time -- a far-off idyll known as the early '90s -- in which show creators could hide behind the conventional wisdom that if you sold a television pilot, the next step was to re-create the pilot at least 13 more times in episodic form in order to make sure everybody "got it"... especially occasional viewers who didn't watch the show from week to week. The result was a comfortable repetition -- TV shows could serve the function of a restaurant where you could always get a table.

Part of me thinks that there still is -- and will always be -- a place for that, but not only is it not the norm anymore, even the most traditionally-formatted of series have been forced to accept a measure of risk in their storytelling in order to remain relevant. Nowadays, risk, as James T. Kirk so aptly put it, "is our business."

Or at least it should be.

Whether people like the show or not, I have seen more risky decisions implemented on *Lost* in two seasons than in the aggregate of most of the shows I have worked on (with the possible exception of *Boomtown*, whose very form was a risk in and of itself). Watching *Galactica* as a fan -- and it is one of only three television series that make me forget that I work in television and cause me to shut down my critical faculty -- the emotion I feel most of the time is "OH MY GOD! DID THEY JUST...?"

Which brings me to the sole reason I am writing this.

The second season finale of *Battlestar Galactica*, "Lay Down Your Burdens." As a TV fan, this is, without a doubt, the best, and most shocking, I have experienced since "The Best of Both Worlds" (the third season finale of *Star Trek: The Next Generation*) in 1990.

Is it shocking because characters are being bumped off? Because it has a cliffhanger I can't imagine the producers writing their way out of (what the promos for *Star Trek* used to call "SHOCKING DESTINY!")? Because it has a twist ending I never saw coming?

No. it's shocking because it simply and effortlessly moves story and character forward -- well beyond what most consider the franchise of the series -- with a sense of inevitability that makes you yearn for, and mourn the loss of, the status-quo at the same time it makes you hunger for what will come next.

Inevitability has become a catchphrase for me as of late. I have come to the realization that plan or no plan, it is the one thing that all good storytelling has in common. Stories can unfold in an infinite number of ways: the job of the storyteller is to convince the audience that the way in which the story being told has unfolded is the only way it could.

After watching "Lay Down Your Burdens" all I can say is that the argument has seldom been made so convincingly.

In a way, the need of some people to know that an all-encompassing plan exists is a need for an upfront assurance of that inevitability. I don't blame them for wanting that -- it's a 500 channel universe, the last thing you want is to miss out on something because you put yourself in the wrong hands.

But, frankly, TV watching is an act of faith, much

as we may want to hedge our bets. When that faith is rewarded, the results are extraordinary, and the form reaches novelistic heights it is only now beginning to truly explore. The consistent achievement of the inevitable born out of great risk may just be the final proof of the true art of television...

And if and when I create my own series, my answer to the question of "Do you have a plan?" will be the equally pointed "Do you have faith?"

THE SHOT BRINGS
YOU BACK

Originally published December 22, 2005, on Livejournal, in apropos of the release of Peter Jackson's remake of King Kong.

The following rant may contain spoilers for *King Kong* (1933, 1976, and 2005 versions).

I didn't hate the new *King Kong*.

I didn't love it either. It may just be the case study for the famous Alfred Hitchcock quote that the length of a film should be directly related to the capacity of a person's bladder. *King Kong* is a masterfully produced entertainment that is nevertheless JUST too darn long for its own good -- and for its own ambitions.

That much said -- and I do think there is a legitimate beef to be had with *King Kong's* running time (more than the combined running time of the original, and *Son of Kong* with much of the first act of *Mighty Joe Young* thrown in for good measure) -- when I see reports on the trades and general media that *King Kong* didn't open as hugely, on a Wednesday night, as expected, I have to ask myself -- are you people just being thick for the sake of an angle?

Seriously -- either the media (classically desperate to brand things as failures or successes based on their performance straight out of the gate -- especially when it's the next film for an Oscar-winning director) is in dire need of a narrative or the studios have forgotten something they have always known. Going to see a three-hour-long film on a school night is not all that palatable even to dyed-in-the-wool geeks like myself. How did they expect it to sit with a general audience?

The near-capacity holiday crowd with which I saw the film last night seemed to enjoy a three-hour break from shopping, and by all indications, the box-office is picking up. So let's stop pretending this is the first long film ever released. Lay off Peter Jackson -- seriously, we need not worry so much about his ability to maintain his voluminous wealth and power. The audience will show up for three hours -- just not when there's a work day on the other side!

Now that I have duly reassured you that *King Kong* is not going to be a flop -- just like it takes a little longer to watch than the average movie, it's going to take a little longer to make its money back -- and Peter Jackson will still be able to afford his second home, let us all sigh in relief and move on to more important topics...

King Kong left me feeling empty. There are several reasons -- one of them has been talked about endlessly, but I feel it cannot be reiterated enough. CGI abuse is a serious problem in our filmmaking culture.

This is not going to turn into a Luddite rant... but I will say this: I spent much of my childhood waiting for that great moment I read about in *Starlog* magazine, as well as much of the mainstream media of the time -- that great confluence of technology, artistry and finance when "filmmaking would catch up to George Lucas's vision" and "he would finally be able to render the totality of the *Star Wars* universe exactly as it existed in his wildest imagination..."

You know what? The day came. Within my lifetime. And I'm not finding it the paradise I was promised.

There is a shot -- THE shot -- that best exemplifies the corrosive effect of unlimited power (and I mean that in terms of the unlimited power to show whatever a director wants on the screen... but I also mean Ian McDiarmid shouting "UN! LIMIT! TED! POW! WAH!" right before fragging Samuel L. Jackson in *Revenge of the Sith*).

It is a shot in which the camera either rises from the ground, or spins around as if it were mounted on a helicopter to reveal a massive fantastical landscape / ancient ruin / vista of Gotham City -- usually crowded with soldiers, Orcs, Stormtroopers or mobs of Mayans / Egyptians / Kryptonians.

(You have also experienced the fraternal twin of "the shot" in a myriad of science fiction / space operas -- it's called "pulling out of a spaceship / futuristic building / space station / fantasy citadel window occupied by real people into the visually stunning synthetic science-fictional / outer space environment outside.")

You know "the shot" because even though CGI as a filmmaking technology is still in a relative state of infancy, you have already seen it a million times. While the rendering and detail work have gotten better over the years, "the shot" is essentially the same... and it still yanks you out of the story because it has no context within the physical reality we inhabit: it doesn't look like it could have been generated by anything other than a computer -- a devastating irony for a technique most often used to establish a location and period...

As a viewer, you want to believe in the magic of "the shot" -- everyone goes to the movies hoping to be beguiled -- but the camera moves a little too smoothly. The buildings look too "designed." The "randomness" of the crowds feels a little too... calculated.

"The shot" is a visual trope that filmmakers abuse because they mistakenly feel it shows the breadth of their vision... but all it really shows is how far the workstations at Skywalker Ranch/WETA/Digital Domain have come since the days of *Tron* and *The Last Starfighter*.

More damningly, abuse of "the shot" in all of its variants is an indicator of a problem endemic to modern film: an inability to keep the story in the here and now of the characters in favor of vistas so sweeping and full of elements that they are rendered meaningless in their excess of visual information.

Good movies, bad movies and fair to middling movies have all featured some version of "the shot" since the inception of CGI -- *King Kong*, *Lord of the Rings*, the *Star Wars* prequels, the *Mummy* movies, *Gladiator,* the *Matrix* trilogy, *The Chronicles of Riddick*, the *Star Trek* TV series and spinoff films...

And we are all the worse for it.

One of the movies I best remember as establishing a cogent, sustained, and infinitely mesmerizing fantasy environment (one that holds up for me having seen it as teenager and adult) is Terry Gilliam's *Brazil*.

Gilliam's screenplay originally opened with a massive special-effects sequence in which building-sized harvesters destroyed a forest in the countryside. In one continuous sequence, the trees cut down by the harvesters were mashed up in gargantuan steampunk combines which sent wood pulp shooting through ducts to the city, where it was collected in great machines that turned it into paper -- the system ultimately spewed the paper forth into trucks which transported the reams into the city, where it was fed into printing machines busily stamping out copies of a government report on environmental conservation.

In short -- it was "the shot."

For all of its potential satiric punch, Gilliam's original opening strikes me as a bit ham fisted and -- more importantly -- as having nothing to do with his characters or story.

I like to think he realized this and thought better of it, but I do worry that -- had he been given access to today's technology when he was making his film -- "the shot" might have stayed on, story relevance be damned.

Instead, Gilliam settled for a relatively modest scene of a bureaucrat swatting a fly. The fly falls into a printer and mucks up the warrant order being processed, resulting in the arrest of an innocent man -- thus creating the inciting incident of the movie. We then see the arrest, and meet the film's leading lady -- who spends the rest of the film trying to free the wrongfully condemned man.

Ultimately, we do get to see Gilliam's 1985, lo-tech, pre-CGI version of "the shot"... a tracking one-take set piece that travels through an office, showing the hustle and bustle in the Orwellian bureaucracy in which the film takes place.

With choreography, clever production design, and a good dolly operator, Gilliam accomplishes everything "the shot" ever tries to do... and manages to truly give a sense of the world his characters inhabit in a very visceral "you are here" kind of way that I have yet to see anyone accomplish with "the shot."

This is not to say that "the shot" was entirely impossible back then. Certainly, Gilliam could have sunk a significant piece of his effects budget into a couple of motion control / traveling matte / cel animation set pieces. There are, in fact, some very impressive synthetic visuals in *Brazil*.

However, like so many other movies unencumbered by the infinite flexibility of CGI -- and infinite flexibility is a greater liability than the most draconian of limitations, in my creative experience -- Gilliam had to plan his shots a little more carefully up front and build his film around what was possible in a much more measured and considered way than filmmakers seem to today.

If you have seen *Lost in La Mancha* or know anything about the making of *Brazil,* you know that holding Terry Gilliam up as a "model of self-control" may be stretching things a little... but in the case of *Brazil*, the result of these exigencies is a greater integration between the story and character content of the film and the visual effects.

To me, the best case study in the perils of unlimited visual power is any direct contrast/comparison between the narrative integrity and emotional import of the *Star Wars* prequels and the original trilogy. One set of films is the work of a director who needed to plan everything down to the detail, working organically -- and in a linear fashion -- all on a basis of serving character and story in order to squeeze the most out of every available shot. The other is the work of a filmmaker whose technology allows him to add entire set pieces to his films in post-production, drop characters into scenes even if they were never filmed (or scripted) that way, and to basically reshape the entire narrative structure of his story after the writing, planning, and principal photography are through.

Ultimately, I am not against the use of CGI. That would be disingenuous, especially coming from a television writer whose first gig was on the first television show ever to have a dedicated, in-house CGI division.

CGI has opened up television and feature films immensely -- and I wouldn't imagine standing here and telling you that Willis O'Brien's gorilla work in the original *King Kong* was "better" than WETA's work on the remake's titular ape. They are both successful applications of an extant technology to create character, which is the cornerstone of good storytelling.

(Although both are superior to the big guy in the 1976 remake... and to the Kong in the Universal Studios Tour, which does, however, have the added perk of being three dimensional and blasting out a thickly scented cloud of "banana breath" every time he roars at your tram, which is a nice touch.)

And that leaves us with a very realistic giant ape...

To Peter Jackson's credit, *King Kong* features things I have never -- ever -- seen (and I have seen some things). As entertained as I was by the film, however, I also spent a lot of time scratching my head and wondering "Wow, how could Ann Darrow (Naomi Watts' character, standing in for Fay Wray) possibly survive THAT?"

(Not to mention the secondary but equally important "Just what is the negligee Ann Darrow wears throughout the vast majority of the film made of anyway -- Kevlar?)

Which brings me to a second issue with modern visual effects in general -- they aid in the creation of what I call "non-survivable events." Now, this is not the sole province of CGI-dominated cinema: I remember a lot of people yelling "LAME!" in the theater when Indiana Jones, Short Round and Willie Scott survived the mine cart jump off the broken-rail cliff.

I also remember thinking those people were lame and had no sense of fun or magic in their lives... but I was 14 at the time and I was willing to accept certain things.

As a 36 year-old, I need for a filmmaker to court my suspension of disbelief . As much as filmmakers have always had the ability to create non-survivable events in cinema (as any fan of Hong Kong action film fight choreography will tell you) CGI allows for non-survivable events to be rendered in such amazing detail that they leave me begging the question as opposed to accepting the reality.

So even though I was amazed by the ever-escalating action of the middle portion of *Kong*, a tonnage issue set in after a while. I started asking myself "How many more times can a giant ape throw a skinny blonde chick in a negligee up into the air and then catch her off a 50 foot drop before she ruptures and herniates a disc?"

(I herniated and ruptured a disc a few years back, so I do have my own preoccupations, I admit.)

(I also have to wonder why, when I saw the *King Kong* coming attractions preview, I found myself so wowed by the shot of Kong tossing Naomi Watts up into the air and then catching her -- I suppose that as an isolated incident, seen once in a montage, it was pretty sweet -- after seeing it repeated over and over again in the film over the course of a very lengthy action sequence, it just loses its impact.)

And so, after watching a virtuosically constructed sequence -- 30 or more minutes of screen time in which I saw a giant gorilla fight off multiple giant iguanas, and people getting caught up in a brontosaurus stampede, and the giant gorilla fighting multiple dinosaurs while dangling hundreds of feet over a chasm before fighting giant-fanged vampire bats, and people fighting giant insects that looked like uncircumcised penises with teeth, and people fighting giant roaches, and people fighting giant grasshoppers and people fighting giant spiders -- I found myself thinking one thing...

None of it was as satisfying as when Indiana Jones

climbed up on that truck and smashed one Nazi's head into the dashboard.

Yes, 14-year-old me just crawled out of my head to tell 36 year-old me that he sucks and should stop being an old fogey. "Chill out," he just said, urging me to accept the reality of modern storytelling and go with the flow.

But the overload got to 36 year-old me. The sheer lack of reality -- of gravity and the laws of physics, even as they pertain to the location of the camera -- wore me down. I was ultimately left with the overwhelming desire that more had been done with less, that the filmmakers, in their zeal to deliver greater thrills hadn't lost sight of the fragility of human beings -- and in doing so, given me a greater respect for those moments in which their lives are endangered and they accomplish something impossible.

I mean, Indiana Jones really, really WORKED to get in the cab of that truck... hard... and when he finally got his mitts on that Nazi, it was cathartic.

I didn't feel that once in *King Kong*.

I remember Terry Gilliam once saying in an interview words to the effect that America robs you of your dreams and replaces them with its own. While that statement says a lot about that particular expatriate artist's political and philosophical world view, it also says a lot about the state of a film industry so technologically advanced in its ability to show it all that it seems to have lost sight of the equally crucial need to show you a little less -- to allow your own imagination to work its own kind of magic...

Because one of the best things a filmmaker can give you is not just dreams (or nightmares) but an experience that opens your mind to new possibilities outside of the screen. Even if the current crop of CGI abusers seems to think they are immune from the responsibility that comes with unlimited power, there is one simple aesthetic principle against which they will ultimately all crash...

Movies just shouldn't leave you wanting less.

EMMY NIGHT

Originally published September 19th and 20th, 2005, on Livejournal in apropos of Lost's Best Drama Series Emmy award win.

PART ONE

A lot of people have asked me what was the highlight of my weekend. Of course, I reply, it was going to LA's famous Arclight Cinema to see *Lord of War*...

OK. Kidding.

Where to begin... actually it all began two weekends ago when, knowing that I was going to be called upon to wear formal attire at the Emmy ceremony, I took a trip to Little India village in Artesia -- guided by *Lost* script wallah extraordinaire and local Bollywood maven Gregg Nations.

I have always wanted a true formal Nehru-style suit -- why? Because Western-style menswear is pathetically limited in variety. I personally think we could all take an example from our friends in the East and dress like we're happy to be alive, instead of on our way to bury our loved ones.

Anyway, this was my opportunity to do it up like a Mumbai movie mogul. So, after a magnificent feast of southern Indian food, Gregg was kind enough to steer us to Raanjha -- a seriously awesome menswear emporium.

Soon, the good people of Raanjha had me set up

with the two best items you will find in my closet... the
more conservative jodhpuri suit I wore to the Emmys
last night, and a long coat with a Nehru-style collar (it
looks like Neo's garment from the *Matrix* sequels, only it
has an intricate black embroidery down the front (paired
with a silver metallic scarf). How awesome is it? Pretty
awesome. In the future, while wearing this garment, I plan
to introduce myself as Neo's more fabulous twin brother
"Leo."

Thus decked out (the spousal unit had a stunning
Herve Leger dress, which, interestingly, enough led to
more of the usual thing that happens when people who
know me meet my wife for the first time -- their eyes bug
out and they exclaim "SHE'S BEAUTIFUL!" -- what they
mean, of course is "HOW IN SAM HILL DID A DORK
LIKE YOU GET THIS LUCKY?")... we patiently waited
down the days to the big event.

I spend Sunday morning in my office "working" (who
are we kidding -- I rearranged my iTunes and iPhoto
libraries for four hours) until the wife comes to get me an
hour before time-to-go, the look in her eye making it very
clear that I probably shouldn't be sitting in my office in a
bathrobe rearranging my iTunes just now.

The limo arrives promptly at three, driven by the
lovely Meghan. Meghan was my driver for the first --
and thus far, only -- *Lost*-themed Creation Convention in
Beautiful Downtown Burbank (our corporate overlords
sprang for the limo then) and was such a swell person that,
when I decided to hire a limo for this event (believe it or
not, going around in limousines is not a common thing
for me, and considering the cost, it isn't likely to any time
soon) I asked for her by name -- which was a good thing
because we spent much of the way back talking about

Battlestar Galactica.

The ride to the Shrine Auditorium should be about
15 minutes, but takes 40 because the last two blocks are
a parking lot of limousines. As we drive in front of the
Radisson Hotel before the Shrine (my alma mater, USC, is
on the other side of the street), I toy with the idea of rolling
down the window, and shouting that I am Robin Williams
(I have been told I look something like him) to see if that
greases the skids any.

The spousal unit talks me out of it.

Another highlight of the ride to the Shrine is the
parade of fundamentalist picketers next to the guy passing
out free CD demos of his music to any limo that passes by
-- which is probably not a bad way to get noticed. Anyway,
according to these fundamentalist picketers, "Hollywood
spreads homo sex," and "the wages of sin is death." Good
to know I have an agenda so hidden even I don't know it.

Also, one of the placards warns us not to "worship
Hollywood posers," which, unlike the first two, is a
perfectly reasonable piece of advice.

At length, Meghan drops us off at the red carpet and I
notice a swell of applause and cheering. The dedicated fan
club for *Lost* writers must be here in force! That or Donald
Trump is standing behind me.

Uh, yeah. Number two.

The wife and I are rushed into a little tent where they
pre-screen arrivals. They need to know when nominees
have arrived in order to alert both security and the
assembled army of press.

A clipboard-wielding woman rushes up to ask if I am
a nominee. I tell her I am. She looks at me funny, like she
can't quite place me (or maybe she was processing how
much different Robin Williams appears in person) and asks

my name, so I reply "Javier Grillo-Marxuach."

She stares at me.

Like I just asked her to lick my face.

In the Klingon language.

Now, I am used to this because of my unusual foreign name, but I figure I might try to spell it for her so she can cross it off her clipboard or whatever it was she had to do -- but the look on her face is one of such confusion and derision that, frankly, I am a bit stuck.

Seriously, she has no idea what to do with me -- then her vision finds someone else slipping by her in a tuxedoed blur. She picks up a walkie-talkie and shouts into it -- like her life is at stake -- that CHRISTIAN SLATER IS ON THE CARPET! HE'S ON THE CARPET!

Then she lets me through with a dismissive wave of the hand.

Lesson learned, let the actors do the on-camera work. Skipping the red carpet.

We walk into the auditorium lobby -- which is crowded and very hot, as it is the only place where drinks are being served. Someone offers us a program.

Now, I gotta confess, I normally hate programs. You go to an event and then you sit and you have to worry about what you do with the program. Under the seat? Sit on it? Do you fold it? Crease it? Seriously, what?

So the wife turns to me and says, "We only need one for the both of us, right?"

Thankfully, my usual disdain for excess paperwork was not in full force. I remind her that this was my first and only Emmy nomination after 10 years of writing for television and 12 in the business as a professional. We'll take two, thank you very much. In fact, we resolve to come back and grab a few more if there's any leftovers.

Ahhh... the Shrine Auditorium: my last time here was 1993... graduation from the Masters Degree program at the USC School of Cinema-Television. I take that as a good omen. Also, it was a cool graduation because the processional was the "throne room" theme from *Star Wars* -- which I guess means that if I succeed to give the school enough money sometime down the line, they might play the haunting *Love Theme from* The Middleman for graduating students. One can dream, right?

After much schmoozing we find our seats. I have an aisle (also a good omen), behind Carlton Cuse. Tomorrow, he will tell me that I left him deaf in one ear -- and perhaps a little dubious of my loyalty -- with my cheers for the nomination of *The 4400*. What can I say? I stick up for my sci-fi brethren.

Naveen Andrews walks by us, and I congratulate him. Naveen and I not only work together on *Lost* but also on a pilot I produced a few years ago -- for which he, surprisingly, has not disowned me. He responds by giving me a big kiss on the cheek.

Some will envy that. Suffer.

The show? Weird. A blur.

Donald Trump sings the theme from *Green Acres*. I get to see William Shatner recite the preamble from *Star Trek*. They show a montage of those who passed on this year, including a few writers... and I fear that when I die, they will flash a really bad picture of me and cite only *seaQuest DSV* as my notable contribution.

Awards are handed out. Everyone looks beautiful in their finery.

As the night wears on, I lose all confidence that we may win. It's not like I walked in thinking we were a shoo-in or anything, but I thought we had a good chance, even for a first-year genre show.

However, as the litany of nominees and winners goes by, I notice that some of the choices are way off the beaten path... and some are totally unexpected... and some are very conservative... and there's nothing wrong with that (what's wrong with making people earn their dues? Far be it for an upstart show like ours to believe we deserve the Emmy when a show like 24 has been out there doing audacious, form-breaking TV for four years).

In short, it's hard to pick out a pattern in who is winning and who is losing -- everything seems recondite and unpredictable.

Also, it's kind of warm and uncomfortable -- and while you at home get to watch commercials, or go to the fridge, we just sort of sit there in these weird, awkward silences with nothing going on onstage. People get up and go to the bathroom or for drinks and schmoozing, etc.

Then -- at the very end of this very long and uncomfortably balmy evening during which we are not exactly effortlessly graceful and glamorous, but more like amateurs acting the part of glamor for the occasional camera angle in our direction -- Wolverine and Guinan from *Star Trek: The Next Generation* get onstage.

(Don't let the song-and-dance-man act fool you -- it was Wolverine, down to the mutton chops.)

And as Guinan and Wolverine go about the interminable task of reciting the names of the nominees for Best Drama Series...

I'm petrified.

The room gets very small. Very crowded. I wonder if I have some kind of late-onset agoraphobia. I tried to go into this with no expectations, but I'd be lying if I told you that the possibility of winning didn't matter.

In fact, in the swirl of all this excitement, it suddenly become the most important thing in the world. I am surrounded by people I respect and admire -- Damon, Carlton, Leonard, JJ, Burky, Thom Sherman, Sarah Caplan, Jean Higgins, Jack Bender, David Fury and the rest of the cast and producers -- and I want to see that group up there, I want to see them smile and be happy. I want to be a part of it. How could I not feel that way?

Too bad we weren't going to win.

No seriously, this is Jack Bauer's year, my rational mind tells me... while my reptile brain screams that I WILL MURDER A PONY TO WIN! I LOVE TO WIN! WINNING IS EVERYTHING! SEXUAL FAVORS ARE <u>NOT</u> OFF THE TABLE! WIN! WIN! WIN!

That's when Wolverine says the word *Lost*.

Before I get to the walk down the red carpet, there are a few observations I'd like to share...

Going to the Emmy awards has a bit of a "this is your life" quality to it. The TV community is a small group, and you are bound to see a lot of people with whom you have worked before. Sitting a few seats over I saw Bryce Zabel -- TV Academy President and creator of *Dark Skies*. Bryce was kind enough -- or was it "brave" enough -- to give me one of my first jobs after *seaQuest* was cancelled and I was certain that I would never work again. He extends his congratulations.

Neil Baer, who once gave me a freelance script on *Law & Order: SVU,* walks by and we exchange greetings. Zack Estrin -- and old comrade from *Charmed* and now a showrunner in his own right -- is there with his father, who is also nominated for an award. An NBC executive steps up to say hello to Damon -- and then to me (he got his start at the network as my assistant some 13 years ago).

There's also a few other people here for whom -- or with whom -- I have worked in the past and who took the opportunity to visit a great deal of madness rage and abuse on me. Weirdly, my being here doesn't feel like a vindication: their presence still raises my sphincter factor to 10.

Basically, wherever I go there is someone I have worked with, or for -- or who has fired me -- at some point.

Similarly, there were a lot of people I have met socially or in the course of doing business other than staffing on shows. Rene Echevarría, for example. He's an awesomely talented writer/producer whom I first met when I was an executive and tried -- laughably -- to recruit him from *Star Trek* onto *seaQuest DSV*. Being a smart man, he turned me down, had an almost decade-long career at *Star Trek: The Next Generation* and its spinoff *Deep Space Nine*, and has been kind enough not to hold against me the truth that my offer would have probably derailed his career and damaged his reputation beyond repair.

Also, in an unrelated observation: there is a simple truth of show business that some people are smaller than life, some are just life size and others are way, way larger.

Terry O'Quinn: larger than life -- a Zen master with a relaxed countenance and an easy grin. Trump -- definitely larger than life, and twice as ugly. Dick Wolf -- way larger than life: looks like he should be commanding an Ayn Randian empire of copper mines and railroads.

Joan Rivers: No metric exists to gauge her relation to life as we know it.

Charlize Theron and Halle Berry: Dear Lord. What if I told you that the camera does them no favors? That as beautiful as these women are on film, in person they are like a D&D character with 32 level charisma?

Seriously -- if you played AD&D and remember the old *Deities and Demigods* handbook, there was one Demigod in there who was "so beautiful that any character who chances upon it is involuntarily falls to their knees in worship."

Yeah. That's the level of inscrutable physical beauty I'm talking about.

And this is not just me being lecherous. The wife agrees. Now, I don't have an opinion about these women as actors one way of the other -- I've seen them both in things I liked and didn't like -- but seeing them in person, I had to ask myself: am I in the same species? 'cause I'm not feeling so pretty myself!

Anyway -- where was I?

Oh, yes, the moment Wolverine calls out the word *Lost*. I yell "HOLY SHIT!"

I wish I had been a little more dignified, but hey, that's how I roll.

I kiss the spousal unit so hard that I leave a permanent mark.

I leap out of my seat.

(I'd like to add that I am not entirely proud of this behavior -- from the time I was a kid I always wondered if the winners were putting on an act for the camera. Could they truly be THAT excited? Now I bear witness... they are.)

The next thing I know I am hugging Carlton Cuse. Then Leonard Dick. Then God knows who -- I think I reached forward, grabbed the back of Damon's head and kissed him on the top of his skull.

We're walking to the podium. JJ and Damon are having a conversation at the foot of the stairs. Later I will find out that JJ was asking Damon to give the acceptance speech

-- it was always assumed that JJ would do the honors, but being the magnanimous guy that he is, JJ felt that Damon should be the one.

Now I'm on stage. My thoughts at that moment...

Oh, what am I talking about? What thoughts? My brain is a hamster on Red Bull and meth. Here is a sample of my brain activity during any given nanosecond and at the same time I was up there:

I wouldn't be here if UPN hadn't cancelled Jake 2.0 *in the middle of its run! Thank you Tyra Banks for doing twice our first run number on a rerun of* America's Next Top Model*! How is my wife going to find me after this? I AM HERE FOR THE GLORY OF QU'ONOS! Do I get my own trophy? God, I love monkeys. The castaways should find a monkey and train it to be their butler. Wolverine! SNCKT! Monkey butler. Chips would be nice. Never be ru-uude to an Arab! Hey -- that's JJ Abrams! Volare! Whoa-oh! E Cantare! I remember a small band of three men I saw while vacationing in the island of Bequia, they sang badly and their instruments were out of tune -- but they had HEART! Shatner was just here! Yeah. Shatner. The Captain. Some dip would be nice with those chips. Hey Guinan? Where's the rest of the El-Aurian refugees? I AM HE AND YOU ARE HE AND HE IS WE AND WE ARE ALL TOGETHER!*

It is a little-known fact that if you stay within three feet of the microphone during the Emmy acceptance speech, you are in the TV zone and will be seen by the folks at home. Since my parents were watching and admonished me to be visible, I planted myself in the safe zone and stayed there until Guinan and Wolverine ushered us out.

Then it gets weird...

You are whisked backstage. Wolverine gets on the X-Jet out of there. Guinan leaves the space-time continuum before you can make her answer for the rest of the El-

Aurian refugees.

Now it's dark. Strange, shrouded figures in headsets whisper-scream for us to move along. All I can see is Emilie de Ravin, who definitely ranks in my list of the "cutest humans alive" (the top ten? My wife, my wife, my wife, my wife, my wife, my wife, my wife, my wife, my wife, and, rounding out the list, my wife).

I only met Emilie once before at a convention. She was not in "House of the Rising Sun" and that was the one of my episodes for which I made the trek to the set of *Lost* in Hawaii. However, she seems to recognize me and we exchange congratulations. Then I notice a light ahead -- a glowing, almost magical beacon of truth...

Mary Hart.

Now we're on *Entertainment Tonight*. Apparently, they have a deal with the TV Academy and the first interview you give after winning is their exclusive right. Having learned my lesson on the red carpet, I try to stay behind the scenes and ask the actors to get up in front of me. Mostly I look at my compatriot Leonard Dick and repeat "Can you believe this?" until the sentence loses all meaning.

Mary Hart is quickly done with us -- the amoeboid blob that is the cast and producers of *Lost* moves to another little staging area. This is where *EXTRA* has their interview set-up. Apparently, they have a deal where they get everyone second after Mary Hart has had her way with them.

Again, I move to the back.

This area is also where the Emmys are handed out. Literally, there's a buffet table full of them and all you have to do is sign! I wondered what was stopping anyone from signing my name and taking one...

Now I have her in my hands!

The Emmy!

The hallowed electron-winged babe herself!

She's heavy and the wings come to two sharp points that could pierce the flesh. No, really, I saw it happen! I think I am going to stick lemons on the tips of mine just to make sure no one is hurt in the future.

And how the hell am I going to find my wife now that I am going deeper into the backstage labyrinth?

EXTRA is done with us. The amorphous blob of *Lost* moves to another area: the picture stage. This is where all the pictures you have seen of us and the actors holding Emmys were taken.

It's a little like Thunderdome.

There's a narrow, catwalk-like stage about three feet wide and 15 feet long -- backed by a graphic with a pattern of Academy logos -- against a set of tiered risers occupied entirely by photographers.

The pictures SNAP a mile a minute. The entire room strobes like some epileptic seizure-inducing Anime kids show. The photographers scream at us:

LOOK OVER HERE! NO OVER HERE! HEY! WRITER BOY! YOU'RE IN FRONT OF EVANGELINE! GET THE HELL AWAY FROM HER! GET OFF THE STAGE FATBOY, YOU'RE BLOCKING MY SHOT OF EVANGELINE! NO -- LOOK OVER HERE! I SAID YOU'RE BLOCKING MY SHOT OF EVANGELINE!

And then something remarkable... one of the photographers must be a member of the aforementioned dedicated fan club for the writers of *Lost* because he calls out my name!

Damon and Carlton look at me in utter shock -- and perhaps wonder who my publicist may be (I don't have one, by the way).

Things settle down (to the extent that they do). We lend the actors our Emmys so that they may pose with them, then get them back for some pictures of our own (Josh Holloway took mighty good care of my little lady -- he's a fine young man!).

OK, *Lost* people -- move on, quickly! Felicity Huffman is on her way in!

Now we're on the official Emmy photography stage. Unlike the previous stage, which is open to all members of the press, this is where the Academy's designated photographers takes pictures for its in-house magazine and gallery.

This "stage" is about the size of an office cubicle and the amoeboid blob of *Lost* consists of over twenty people.

The photographer squeezes us in. I wind up sitting on a ledge of the two-tiered stage with my back up against JJ's knees. It's a weird employer bonding experience. At one point, JJ puts his Emmy on my head.

And it looks GOOD on me!

Next!

Now we're in the general press area -- Thunderdome #2. This is where print, wire and local media get their quotes for the next morning's stories about the event. It's another upraised dais with a line of microphones delineating the stage from the 10-rows-deep cluster of reporters serving the inquisition.

Again, I stick to the back and let the cast, JJ, Carlton and Damon be the face of the show.

Besides, I have to go find my wife!

Jeff, a nice guy who works for CBS, escorts me and Leonard Dick (who has also lost his spouse) all the way through the media labyrinth. We fight the Minotaur and emerge back into the auditorium victorious and unscathed -- only the place has been cleared out! I feel like Harrison Ford in *Frantic*: WHERE'S MY WIFE?!?

Time to go outside (and no, I didn't bring my cell phone, the Academy discouraged it). Soon we get to the red carpet area find our wives... whom we must then escort right back through the labyrinth to where we left the amoeboid blob of *Lost* people , just as they wrap up in the general press room.

Jeff, if you are reading this, you are a *mensch*, and may have saved my marriage from one of those ugly "you hit it big and left me behind" arguments you hear in 1930s melodramas about Hollywood.

Now we enter the last level of the labyrinth. It's a large area where all the major media have set up tents (also about the size of an office cubicle) for live, post-show interviews. The TV Guide Channel. *Extra* (again). *The Insider* (and they win for weirdest booth -- not only did they have Pat O'Brien standing in front of a piano, for a Sinatra vibe, I guess, but also making the place even more cramped and hot -- they have these acrylic doors that SLAM! shut automatically when he starts interviewing the amoeboid blob, making sure no one can escape!).

Since I am in the back and at no risk of media exposure, I turn and look through the acrylic doors at my wife -- alternately making fish faces or pretending to try to beat through them with my Emmy (kind of like Dustin Hoffman in *The Graduate*).

She is not amused.

OK, so Pat O'Brien is done with the amoeboid blob of *Lost*...

A word about the Pat O'Brien experience, and celebrity in general. I don't feel like judging O'Brien in his recent travails -- the embarrassing exposure of sexually harassing voice messages he left to female co-workers -- but I must say that it is a strange experience when you are in the same space as someone whose troubles you have read about in tabloids and whose secrets have been made public. It's like being in an uncanny valley where the person in front of you is at once completely familiar in the least comfortable way possible and yet a complete stranger.

In short, if anyone ever tells you that television doesn't give you a strange and completely false sense of intimacy with the people on the other side, they are wrong.

We are released back into the labyrinth. Now we're at the TV Guide Channel's booth -- then we are on E! -- and their tent is a little larger, so I get a some play in front of the cameras. Some people who watched the post-show would later ask me why I was continually looking up. It's because they had a monitor showing their feed up above the cameras and I was watching the show even as I was in it -- it's like being in a Moebius loop of pure entertainment! I am watching me, while being me while watching me watching myself!

Then comes CNN. Another tiny little room into which some clever set designer put a massive sofa, perhaps in the belief that it would create the illusion of a palatial expanse. I get shoved in behind the sofa along with Emilie and Naveen -- who ultimately stage dives over the sofa to land behind JJ and Damon.

The interviewer asks JJ and the rest of the cast if we are wearing "muted colors" such as black in honor of the victims of Hurricane Katrina.

An uncomfortable silence follows.

I don't want to be the one to say it, but i'm definitely thinking it... uh, lady, we're wearing black because it's a black tie event.

The interview gets more political -- do we think Bush and company did a good job handling Katrina? Do we think celebrities have a responsibility to speak up?

Oh-kay!

Damon gives his best, most polite response along with JJ -- and then there's an awkward silence, like we have not satisfied the needs of this hard-talking news organization. Saving the day, Josh Holloway -- with his unmistakable sloe-drawlin' Southern charm -- makes the case that speaking out is a personal choice, celebrity or otherwise.

The reporter gives us all a thoughtful look. I'm worrying that she is gearing up to ask about the Supreme Court confirmation hearings, or the firing of Michael Brown, or whether the cast and crew of the Emmy Award-winning TV series *Lost* has an official position on the bill on agricultural pesticide subsidies for Central America going up before subcommittee in the House.

Mercifully, Felicity Huffman is on her way, so the interview wraps up in a whimper of awkwardness. The amoeboid blob of *Lost* moves on: consuming all interviewers in its path!

Good Morning America follows. Then *The Today Show*. I must say that at this point, even the most die-hard of hams among the amorphous blob of *Lost* are getting tired. We have now been doing this for an hour and a half and are beginning to wonder whether this awards-show win is really so pivotal a moment in history as to require this depth of coverage.

The amoeboid blob of *Lost* moves on to the Governor's Ball, next door to the auditorium. Where they found the space to stick the Labyrinth of Media I don't know -- I think they pulled a TARDIS on us.

Finally, I get some time with the spousal unit. We wind our way through the Ball. We are on table 510 -- so the distance between the entrance and our table was roughly equal to the width of my ancestral homeland of Puerto Rico...

The "Ten Tenors" sing on stage. When we enter the ball, they are singing a Bee-Gees song. By the time we find our table they are singing an aria from *Figaro*... and I wonder how one would say "is that your jive talking, telling me lies" in Italian, 'cause that would be a neat karaoke trick.

We sit.

I put the Emmy down on the table, alongside the others belonging to Damon, Leonard, and Jack Bender. The dinner is fantastic -- beef Wellington, shrimp cocktail, a frozen fruit dessert thing. It's like the scene in *The Right Stuff* where the test pilots who break speed records get a steak with all the trimmings at Pancho Barnes' Happy Bottom Riding Club... only without the courage, manliness, and aeronautical skill.

Also, I'm so hungry at this point (my sole nourishment for the day was a Jamba Juice about 12 hours before) that I just shovel the stuff into my mouth like Kurt Russell in that movie *Soldier*. Yes, that is the metaphor I have chosen to convey the truth of that moment... can we move on?

My agent stops by to say congratulations. Now more than ever -- in this, the post-*Entourage* era -- agents are treated as objects of ridicule, seen as parasites and called names too unspeakable to be said in polite company. So let me set the record straight. I have been with my agent for over 10 years. He has pushed and encouraged me, seen me through some serious crap, always answered my calls within three hours of my placing them, never ignored a plea for help and talked me off the ledge more often that I care to admit.

This guy is a partner at his agency and even as he has risen in the ranks and gotten his due (and his name on the letterhead) he is still the same guy who used to talk to me three times a day (during one particularly crappy year -- then I got a therapist and, well, haven't had to call as much, which is also good). So, the next time you are watching *Entourage* and are tempted to think that all Hollywood agents are self-serving, supercilious scum, try to think of what I just said.

Or don't and have a good laugh. Who am I to tell you how to live?

The ball is winding down. People are leaving for all of the swank after parties... I have no swank after party to go to, being a dorky writer with a hard-to-spell name. Also, I have to write on my top-secret DC Comics project tomorrow morning before going to work!

Several people tell me that all I have to do is wave my Emmy around like a Golden Ticket and I will be given entrance to any party I wish. Aside from wishing I'd had an Emmy in high school, I am not really all that tempted -- I mean, they didn't want me before, why would I go now. I want them to love me for who I am, not for some statue!

So we grab our programs and our specially packaged Dove chocolates (inside an "Emmy Passport") and head out.

My wife stops to get a coffee at a conveniently located stand near the exit. Yep, we're in LA -- the town lives on coffee now that the '80s are over and cocaine has fallen out of vogue. After much joking about my using the Emmy to replace the eagle on top of the espresso machine, the awfullest truth of this entire night is revealed to us...

They don't have whole milk! Only non fat and 2%! And why? Because there's actors here -- and actors don't drink whole milk, even on nights of celebration.

We settle for 2% and call it a night.

The limousine staging area has been called "the great democratizer." You see, the limo drops you off and gets a number before going off to a nearby parking lot to wait while you win or lose and then get sauced in either celebration or mourning -- then, when the time comes to go, you hand in your number and wait for the limo to return. So, for a good hour, you just stand there -- surrounded by actors, celebrities and personalities, network presidents and even lowly writers.

Everyone has to wait for their limo in turn, just like everybody else. Democracy!

Why do I feel like that metaphor just isn't landing?

Meghan finally drives up and I cross the street to meet the car -- at which time one of the LAPD's finest yells at me to:

"GET OFF THE ROAD YOU STUPID IDIOT! OR DON'T! WHAT DO I CARE IF YOU GET HIT BY A LIMO, YOU JERK!"

This was absolutely no different from how the cops treated me when I jaywalked during my days as a grad student at USC. So it came as a familiar and welcoming tone. Almost like a lullaby.

I'm home by 11:30 P.M.

I guess me and the wife are kind of a pair of homebodies, but we miss our dogs... who meet us with the same joy that they show on days when we don't win Emmys. Or maybe they just have to go outside to take a shit.

I never know.

I check my email -- 75 new messages. I will have returned them all by Tuesday night. I usually suck at correspondence and thank-you notes, but I felt so blessed and lucky to have gotten this award that I wanted to return the courtesy in some greater karmic way.

Then me and the wife just sort of stare at the Emmy on our dinner table for a while, wondering what the hell just happened.

In a few days, I am going to drive the trophy to its permanent home in my parents' house. They will get a lot more pleasure from the award than me -- and that's saying a lot, 'cause I love the living cheese and croutons out of my winged Art Deco beauty -- but hey, they did put me through film school (a risky investment at best) and since I didn't get to thank them on stage, this is a pretty good reminder of how much I appreciate their lifetime of support.

After the gawking at the statue has run its course, I watch the moment of our victory on TiVo -- and realize how little of it I actually remember.

Damon gave a beautiful and heartfelt extemporaneous speech that managed to convey what all of us felt: our tremendous luck for being there -- a first year show that we are proud of, and that has popular success and validation from the establishment, is probably the rarest thing in television, especially in our fragmented media world. We have much for which to be thankful -- not just artistically and commercially, but also personally, as we all have so many others supporting us and seeing us through.

Damon said it best and did us proud.

I watch it over and over again. I study it. I look at my friends and myself. I laugh at the sight of myself, not because of low self-esteem but because, I dunno, I'm giddy and consider myself something of a comical figure up there with my uncertain beard, thinning hair and yellow glasses, and that ridiculous jacket that makes me look like *Dr. No*.

How did they ever allow a clown like me to besmirch the honor of this proud Academy anyway?

(Then I remember that this proud Academy also gave not one but two of these awards to Liberace, so... you know...)

And that's how my Emmy night ended... with me living my own memories through a satellite-enabled digital recorder. As we should all know by now, the only way to truly know that a transcendent moment of triumph and personal accomplishment actually took place is to see it on television.

By the way, *Lord of War* is an awesome movie. I recommend it without reservation.

FUCK YOU, YOU FUCKING FUCK!

Originally published June 7th, 2005 on Livejournal, in apropos of that month's issue of Harper's magazine.

PROLOGUE

A homeless man walks up to a literature professor and asks for dollar. The literature professor declares, "Neither a borrower, nor a lender be -- William Shakespeare." The homeless man replies, "Fuck you, you fucking fuck -- David Mamet."

IN WHICH I INVITE DAVID MAMET TO BITE ME (AND CONSEQUENTLY BIG-MOUTH MYSELF OUT OF THE OPPORTUNITY TO WRITE FOR THE BRAND SPANKIN' NEW SHOW HE JUST CO-CREATED)

I don't usually buy *Harper's* magazine. I'm a little bit too low-falutin' for that kind of goings-on, and frankly, where print media is concerned, I'd rather spend my hard-earned coin on whatever Kurt Busiek is doing nowadays -- but something about the cover of this month's issue called out to me:

"BAMBI V. GODZILLA -- WHY ART LOSES IN HOLLYWOOD"
by David Mamet

Upon closer examination, I realized -- much to my chagrin

and dismay -- that America's Greatest Living Playwright™ was not, in fact, finally paying a much overdue homage to Marv Newland's seminal piece of animated indie cinema.

Nevertheless, I decided to buy the magazine. Probably out of some perverse impulse to dive head-first into the sort of bourgeois cultural criticism that occasionally deigns to look down from its even-better-heeled-than-NPR praise of safe things (a portfolio by David Hockney? Really? Wow! That's shiny!) to comment on the work of My People in the same way that Marlon Perkins used to comment on the animal kingdom.

Not to mention that after 12 years of toiling away in the trenches of Hollywood, I have been waiting all this time for a true Mandarin of the art form to come down from his Forbidden City and explain to me exactly why it is that I suck.

Let me give it to you in short -- since it takes Mamet over a thousand words (and those words include "vizier," "mirabile dictu," and "myrmidons" -- yup, myrmidons* -- *Harper's* must have been paying by the syllable that week) to get to his point...

Corporations are evil. Consolidation and a government-empowered sense of entitlement has only made The Man more nefarious in his pursuit of power. Writers -- being morally superior to just about everyone, including The Man -- have within them the power to create whatever they want: to truly elevate the world with their art. However, artists -- other than David Mamet, who has apparently been to the mountain and seen the Promised Land -- are also naïvely attached to the idea of a mass audience and thus persist in the belief that art is possible

---

*   Don't feel bad, I had to look it up too -- here it is according to dictionary.com: "myrmidon" -- a faithful follower who carries out orders without question.

even in the service of a corporation.

In short, The Man knows that we writers are idealists and uses such weapons as contractual obligation to force us to make shit out of our dreams.

In addition, Mamet makes an Uzi-wielding drive-by at critics, whom he claims are merely in the business of creating meta-narratives of little worth other than to carve out a larger cultural space around the entertainment industry and its product. Thus, Mamet argues, all critics truly do in the grand scheme is aid and abet Hollywood's agenda of cultural genocide by drowning out other, perhaps more worthy, discourse.

In a telling omission, Mamet never deigns to unpack what it means -- in the light of his contention -- when Great Living American Playwrights™ write long articles for general interest publications decrying the hypocrisies of the entertainment business to an audience primarily outside the entertainment business...

Or when they write plays like *Speed the Plow:* a scathing satire of the hypocrisies of the entertainment business... or when they write movies like *State and Main:* a gentle, daffy poke-in-the-ribs of the hypocrisies of the entertainment business... or when they bring their big guns to bear on something like *Wag the Dog:* a blistering polemic on the hypocrisies of the entertainment business...

Or maybe I just mistook *Speed the Plow, State and Main,* and *Wag the Dog* for mere entertainment as opposed to the intended incendiary call to take to the streets and engage in wildcat violence and insurrectionary acts in the name of showbiz reform.

Finally, Mamet also takes a red-hot poker to agents, lawyers and managers, whom he decries as the tools of the evil establishment. In Mamet's view, all of these people are predators of dubious worth whose services exist only to hold the artist down, choke him financially, and keep him indentured to The Man when he should be out there wresting Great Art from the living earth.

Now let me counter my own argument before I even make it...

Being as I am a myrmidon (look ma, I can write!) and not America's Greatest Living Playwright™ I am naturally going to argue that my blind lackeydom to The Man is -- in fact -- my clever use of a mass medium as a tool in a search for Greater Truth. It is in my nature as a deluded writer (or "bovine" as Mamet so delicately categorizes the rest of us) -- unable to give up on my naïve hopes of someday creating high art out of the fodder given me by The Man out of fear of being seen as "a hack" -- to shake my head and cry out "nuh-uh!" in the face of Mamet's awful truth.

And let's face it, I worked for Aaron Spelling, for Christ's sake: how else could I sleep at night if I didn't have it in me to write a treatise not only defending -- but also ennobling -- my own bondage?

Honestly, what kind of cog am I if I can't rationalize the fact that I sold out early -- and often? What kind of slave doesn't eventually buy into the myth that if "I am a good worker bee now, The Man will eventually allow me to do the quality work I always had in me?"

What Mamet's article implies by labeling me a sheep is that if I argue against his central contentions it is because of my own lack of vision: my need to justify to myself my own unwillingness to hate Big Brother, break free from the shackles and create True Art. And by "True Art" I mean something like Mamet's own screenplay for *The Edge* -- which we all know to be the *ne plus ultra* of man-eating bear as an analogy for the demons that plague the weak of spirit.

OK, that was a cheap shot.

But, you know what? I gotta ask myself, reading Mamet's treatise, why exactly is he writing this? It's not breaking news that Hollywood is a machine where individuals have to struggle to create something truly unique. Is he merely offering a fancy-pants commentary as an amusement for those who usually don't sully their hands with popular media? Is he making a call to arms for artists to emancipate themselves from their mental slavery and go to Work?

Seriously. What does the man want for my blood?

Mamet reveals his true agenda rather late in the essay, actually, (in the third-to-last paragraph, in fact) by which time you -- the reader -- may have been too beaten down by the viziers and myrmidons to judge him with the severity he deserves. I quote:

> *"...in my experience, almost every financial interchange with Hollywood ends with an accusation of the corporation of theft: 'you didn't do what I wanted; you didn't work hard enough; you intended to defraud me.' There are the recurring plaints of industry. They may be translated as you forgot to work for nothing. The corporation is enraged that the raw materials it is their charter to exploit have found voice and 'answered back.'"*

Answered back? Really?

See -- it's no secret that David Mamet hates -- hates, hates, hates -- the entertainment industry. He hates producers and he hates studios. On his IMDB page, one of his quotes compares allowing Hollywood to option his material to "raping your kids to teach them about sex."

The curious thing is that it's also no secret that Mamet makes a very good living off the entertainment industry.

Knowing this, it comes as no surprise that -- after all the verbiage -- what Mamet is really pissed-off about is that those loathsome little studio myrmidons often have the temerity to ask that he do the work for which he has agreed to receive the kind of massive fees that could only be paid when America's Greatest Living Playwright™ descends from the gilded boards and deigns to touch the greasy paste that is entertainment for the common folk and, through his touch, elevate it into fine art.

Let's face it -- Mamet may have written *Fool For Love* -- no, wait, that was Sam Shepard, whom I loved as Chuck Yeager in *The Right Stuff* and who seldom writes long essays complaining about how he makes his money.

Ahem.

Let's face it, Mamet may have written *American Buffalo*, but he probably made a crapload more money from the script fees paid for, say, his adaptation of Thomas Harris' pulp serial-killer-as-Nietzchean-superhero-novel *Hannibal* than he will ever make off the royalties from the performance of even his greatest work for the stage.

Now, I don't know if you have read Mamet's adaptation of *Hannibal* but there is a reason why America's Greatest Living Playwright™ was removed from the project and replaced with Steven Zaillian (the Hollywood hack responsible for such garbage as *Searching for Bobby Fischer* and *Schindler's List*).

Mamet's adaptation stank.

It not only stank of poor craftsmanship, it stank of contempt. Contempt for the material (and I can't blame him for that, the book is about as perfunctory a fulfillment of contractual obligation as they come -- but then again, I would have probably turned down the assignment on principle, and continued working for Aaron Spelling), contempt for the audience, and contempt for the people making the film. It is the work of a man hired on reputation to presumably elevate a sub-standard piece of material pissing out a transcription of a bad novel and laughing all the way to the bank.

All of which begs the question: why shouldn't America's Greatest Living Playwright™ cash a paycheck on occasion?

Seriously. The man wrote *Savage in Limbo,* no wait, that was John Patrick Shanley, who won an Oscar for writing *Moonstruck,* whose *Joe vs. the Volcano* I absolutely adored, and who -- to my knowledge -- doesn't write victim-blaming articles for tony publications bemoaning how Hollywood has disrespected him.

Ahem.

Seriously. The man wrote *Oleanna,* why shouldn't he make the occasional cash run?

I mean, it's not like David Mamet shows up every couple of seasons -- or when he has to make a house payment -- at the office of some poor unsuspecting television development wonk, dolled up like an Aztec, bejeweled with the aura of his accomplishments, and promises to write an amazing draft of a great pilot for an incredible series only to turn in the kind of scripts that are never heard from again!

Oh. Wait.

He's done that rather a few times in the past 10 years, actually. Once when I was an executive at a network...

In fact, I remember waiting to receive the first draft

of his pilot with breathless anticipation... hoping to feel the touch of pure genius. I also remember reading the last page of this script, putting it down and...

Well.

Do you remember the movie *A Christmas Story*? When Ralphie sends out for the Little Orphan Annie decoder ring, spends weeks waiting for it in the mail, finally receives it, locks himself up in the family bathroom to decode the secret message... and ultimately discovers that the secret message was an ad for Ovaltine? In one of the truest coming-of-age moments ever committed to film, Ralphie looks up, realizing he has been robbed and, with grim resignation, utters a line made immortal by thousands of Christmas-day showings on TBS:

"Son of a bitch!"

Which brings me back to Mamet.

Clearly, the respect of a fledgling writer moonlighting as a network executive was worth the cost of that house payment. And isn't respect what this is really all about?

Under the weight of so many 25 cent words lies a pretty simple conceit: it's not enough for the Greatest Living American Playwright™ to cash in now and then on his rightfully earned acclaim -- he feels entitled to a measure of respect for his trouble.

After all -- what is more noble than stealing from The Man?

Not to mention that -- after years of kicking around the trenches of television development -- the pilot to which Mamet most recently lent his name and pedigree actually turned out to be a going concern (*The Unit* co-created with *The Shield*'s Shawn Ryan: coming mid-season to CBS).

So -- bonus! Now David Mamet can get a fat Executive Producer fee for the run of the series, hire his own staff of bovines and lecture them about how to create drama, write episodes if and when he wants, and create True Art in his copious free time.

So why, David, do you feel the need to justify your artistic -- and financial -- success with pedantic prose on the pages of *Harper's*?

Hey -- not everyone gets the opportunity to direct films they write -- or to get a series on the air. You make a great living off the entertainment industry, sometimes on projects you love, sometimes on projects you do for the money, just like most of your scribbling brethren...

And sometimes, you may even take money from The Man, because your unique status as America's Greatest Living Playwright™ often blinds The Man into giving you a check for something like your rushed transcription -- ahem, adaptation -- of *Hannibal*, or a handful of pilots that got your name splashed all over the pages of Daily Variety before vanishing into oblivion...

And you know what? That's fine too. You hate The Man -- and everybody knows it now -- you wanna fuck the machine? Knock yourself out! Fuck it! Fuck it blue! You earned it -- you wrote *A Few Good Men* -- ahem... you wrote *The Water Engine* for fuck's sake!

But never forget that you and I suck on the same teat, my good man.

Even if you are the Greatest Living American Playwright™ and I once worked for Aaron Spelling, you are still my colleague, and make your living the exact same way I do. You want my respect? Don't call me a sheep unless you've fed, herded, and shorn me.

And in case you didn't get it, here it is in language Ricky Roma would understand: you got in bed with the devil -- don't complain that you had to fuck!

REQUIEM FOR A NEMESIS

Originally published February 18, 2005, on Livejournal.

In 1994, I was a young, green executive toiling away in the trenches of the National Broadcasting Company. Among my responsibilities as "Manager of Current Series," I was the day-to-day liaison for televisual train-wreck that was *seaQuest DSV*.

My job: to be a point of contact between the Executive Producers of the show and the higher-ups at the network. It was not the easiest job in the world (although there are many worse).

seaQuest DSV was what they charitably call a "troubled" show -- it went through five Executive Producers in two seasons, and underwent a radical change from a relatively ill-conceived attempt to do a semi-realistic adventure in an underwater future to a sensationalistic, almost-anthology series in which the inhabitants of a futuristic submarine -- many of whom barely had the same name and backstory from episode to episode -- faced off against a myriad of creatures, aliens, killer plants (I wish I were kidding) and sometimes even Greco-Roman gods (and those of you who watched *seaQuest DSV* know the surreal truth I'm talking about).

Because of this radical change in subject matter, *seaQuest DSV* became one of the -- if not the -- first shows in television to be subject to something that is now commonplace: an internet fan campaign. In this case, the campaign was run by fans of the first season who felt that the show needed to return to its roots in underwater exploration and fact-based adventure.

Not realizing the floodgate it would open, I answered the fan campaign with an open letter which I thought addressed many of their concerns, attempted to present a realistic picture of what level of change could be expected, and opened a door for fans to contact me personally with their questions, comments and feedback on the show. The woman who ran the campaign -- her name was Mary Feller -- was kind enough to discuss the aims of the campaign with me and post the letter on Usenet and forward the replies. At the time I wrote the letter, I didn't even have an America Online account -- the internet was a vast unknown.

The "Open Letter to the Rescue *seaQuest* Campaign" -- having been written by a rather passionate but also colossally naïve 25-year-old manchild -- was also much more lengthy, pompous (some things NEVER change), and truth-telling in a kind of "look-at-me-I'm-a network-executive-feed-me-Seymour" kind of way than was probably necessary.

That much said, it was a heartfelt attempt to embrace the fan community and to offer an avenue for feedback and communication. Even if my power to affect the future of *seaQuest* was not in any way whatsoever total -- or all that present given my low-level job -- I have always been a genre fan and, from that perspective, thought that it was necessary for fans to feel like theirs was a vital voice that networks ignore at their own peril. I hold that opinion to this day -- and believe that the many successful fan campaigns that have evolved from the internet vindicate that point of view.

Many things that came out of my submitting that open letter to the wild and wooly web, among them...

A newfound appreciation for the power of the internet... several hundred letters from passionate, well-meaning fans who truly wanted the show to succeed, being quoted -- much to my embarrassment and the rage of my superiors -- by *USA Today* in a story about the declining fortunes of a once-promising show... a four-page missive from the great maker himself, J. Michael Straczynski, admonishing me to simply hire "the best writers" and let them go at it without intervention... having one of the Executive Producers of *seaQuest* and at least one Universal studio executive tear me several new sigmoid orifices for speaking publicly on the subject of their show...

And the arrival in my life of the man who would -- over the years -- become my nemesis.

Gharlane of Eddore.

Although Gharlane's true identity was divulged shortly after his death (not spoiling anything here, it's called "Requiem for a Nemesis"), the man jealously protected his anonymity during his lifetime and I feel a debt to honor the way in which he lived his life.

Named after a character in the "Lensman" novels of E. E. "Doc" Smith (whom he apparently knew personally, and whose permission he requested in order to adopt the handle), Gharlane was a self-styled great Brahmin of the World Wide Web. He had posted in everything from the most primitive of bulletin boards to the Usenet of the late 1980s and '90s and had a voluminous history with the medium. He was also an incredibly prolific poster.

In many ways, Gharlane of Eddore was the highly

evolved embodiment of the seminal SF fan. A well-educated, second-amendment-loving libertarian/atheist/contrarian with an encyclopedic knowledge of Pretty Much Everything, tremendously strong opinions (and the sheer tyranny of will to voice them as The Truth), a default contempt for the lesser forms of the genre -- with the exception of those examples which matched his deeply personal convictions of what made for good popular/cheesy entertainment -- and a tremendously idiosyncratic sense of humor (Gharlane did little to discourage the popular myth that his ability to carry on dozens of online arguments simultaneously stemmed from his actually being a tentacled gelatinous cube living in a liquid medium).

Indeed, Gharlane of Eddore saw himself as THE natural enemy of lazy writing and scientific inaccuracy and pursued his pet peeves with predatory ferocity... and he disliked me with a sustained intensity I have not since encountered on the web.

At the root of Gharlane's antipathy (I hate to refer to it as anything more than that -- Gharlane would probably post a scathing comment saying that he was above feeling anything such as "passion" in his distaste for me, that I was merely a fly to be swatted away) was his belief that my letter to the fans of *seaQuest DSV* was deeply insulting -- or, as he put it...

> *"Javier Grillo-Marxuach is famous on the Net for his posting explaining to the 'SinkQuest' fans that it was really a very good, very well-written series, and that their failure to appreciate it was THEIR fault. I don't have a copy of that posting,*

*or I'd paste it in, here; I and friends have
been trying to find a good copy for a couple
of years, since that particular on-line
discussion antedated the creation of most
of the readily-accessible on-line archive
sites. If anyone's got a good copy, preferably
with the original header information, please
post it for the edification of... the rest of the
group; it's jaw-droppingly hilarious, and
a wonderful explication of just why Mr.
Grillo-Marxuach should probably keep his
nose out of the genre."*

Now that Google Groups has caught up in archiving
legacy material from the Bad Old Days, the letter is widely
available, and I will leave it up to you to decide whether or
not Gharlane's interpretation is valid or not. It's probably
not hard to figure out where I fall on that, but as a cultural
studies major who read more post-structuralist literary
analysis than I care to recount, I will defer to the notion
that reception is as important as authorial intent in this
case.

The point is that from the moment my letter hit the net,
Gharlane of Eddore became my A#1 public detractor.

As I transitioned from network executive to
professional writer, things became especially dicey. Every
time I did something, or someone else did something that
merited a comparison to something abjectly mediocre in
Gharlane's eyes, I could count on a barb showing up on
the web.

Here are some of Gharlane's greatest hits:

"Javier Grillo-Marxuach could type a better script with his left foot while dead drunk and watching the Naked People Channel while wearing a lampshade over his head. Of course, that appears to be the way he does most of his work... "

In apropos of my work on *The Pretender*, Gharlane pulled few punches...

"...considering the show's staffing and the network it's on; if NBC doesn't kill it, Javier Grillo-Marxuach will."

Clearly, in Gharlane's cosmology of the entertainment business, I was as powerful an influence on a show I didn't create as the network that bankrolled the series. He either didn't know what it meant -- or chose to ignore for the sake of his world-view -- that I was a mere Story Editor: the second-lowest-ranked level of writer on a staff. Gharlane's ongoing conviction of my pernicious effect on a show was evidenced by statements such as...

"...as long as the likes of Javier Grillo-Marxuach and NBC itself are involved in dictating the content, there's just a whole lot of limit to how far or how intelligently the show can go."

And:

"Well, the major problems with 'THE PRETENDER,' as have been noted

> *elsewhere, are Javier Grillo-Marxuach, and*
> *NBC's corporately-dictated soap-opera*
> *guidelines."*

When I moved on from *The Pretender* to work as the
third-lowest level writer (a promotion!) on another show,
entitled *Three*, Gharlane came right along for the ride
to make sure everyone knew his opinion of me and my
shoddy, derivative work...

> *"Right, now he appears to be the Story*
> *Editor In Charge of Making Sure That Every*
> *Stand-Alone-Story-of-the-Week Looks*
> *Exactly Like Every Other Stand-Alone-*
> *Story-of-the-Week for 'THREE.' Or maybe*
> *Exactly Like Every Stand-Alone-Story-of-*
> *the-Week for 'TEAM KNIGHT RIDER.'"*

As the years went by, Gharlane was kind enough to grant
me the status of some kind of insidious and annoying, yet
insignificant, minor demonic form, as evidenced by this
post...

> *"When you utter Names Of Malign Power*
> *in public, you have to immediately sprinkle*
> *sea-salt in a circle around you, spit three*
> *times over your left shoulder, and repel*
> *malign influences by reciting three times,*
> *very very fast, 'MARTIAL LAW' is even*
> *better than 'DIAGNOSIS: MURDER!'*
> *This confuses them and they go away. Of*
> *course, this won't work against Javier*
> *Grillo-Marxuach. *NOTHING* works*

against Javier Grillo-Marxuach."

(The references to *Diagnosis: Murder* and *Martial Law* were swipes at my friends and fellow writers William Rabkin and Lee Goldberg -- who were Producers on *seaQuest* and have their own history of warfare on the web)

In the fullness of time, Gharlane refocused his efforts on taking on NBC as a bigger target (he despised what he perceived as the network's institutionalized pro-gun control stance) and appeared to cut me some slack when he said...

> *"In short, I have no great love for NBC, and Javier Grillo-Marxuach is the *least* of NBC's offenses against the public weal."*

But this *détente* was short lived...

> *"'Dumbest Post Ever' is still Javier Grillo-Marxuach's impassioned thesis explaining that the folks on the Net didn't have the education or native intelligence to appreciate the magnificence of 'SinkQuest,' and that the problem with the ratings was due to the clod-like lack of perspicacity on the part of the viewers... They're still laughing over *that* one in places ranging from Alaska to Zimbabwe."*

This last post is interesting because it made me so angry that I actually complained about it to an internet-savvy friend at a party. It prompted her to step up to my defense with the following reply...

> *"Oh my God. Gharlane, let it go. Please. The*
> *statute of limitations has run out on this*
> *one. For all that is holy, just let it go. I beg*
> *you."*

To which Gharlane, God bless his tenacity, consistency, and honesty, replied...

> *"Sorry. Besides, I'm still working on*
> *grudges from 1952, why should I cut Grillo-*
> *Marxuach any slack?"*

When I think about Gharlane, I often wonder what it was about him that upset me so much.

He certainly wasn't (and isn't) the only person to ever malign me in a public forum... but his words stung. It doesn't really make much sense, since the guy didn't know me personally or -- in spite of the self-assurance with which he put forth his accusations -- have a particularly good grasp on the circumstances under which most low-level TV executives or writers do their work.

Maybe it just got under my skin that -- during a time when I was struggling to adjust to being a writer on staffs and the autocratic management style of most Executive Producers -- here was someone accusing me of personally dictating content on shows which I neither created nor ran.

Or maybe it was that I perceived the *raison d'être* for Gharlane's feud against me as a deliberate and willful misunderstanding of what I had intended as a gesture of goodwill toward a very disgruntled fan community; the act of a carpetbagger intruding on turf he had established back when the web was just a bunch of trunk lines and dial-up modems.

Or maybe it's just no fun being called a talentless hack.

Another possible explanation is that -- because Gharlane's use of my name as a punch line emerged from my first (not so) baby steps into the world of the internet -- it rankled me deeply that someone could capitalize on the relative anonymity of this then-new medium to publish tremendously incendiary rhetoric about another person without any seeming consequences to their own person.

The "Gharlane of Eddore FAQ" -- still up on the web as a memorial -- makes it clear that Gharlane protected his identity jealously in order to avoid personal harassment by those who disagreed with him. I envy his wisdom: the first time I posted to a public forum, my name wound up on USA Today and I was -- appropriately -- taken to the woodshed by my superiors for embarrassing them by speaking for them and their program in a national publication.

But there is something profoundly disingenuous in my envy. It is, after all, completely possible to write in complete anonymity.

The tone and content of my open letter, as well as my chosen career, makes it clear that I never wanted that for myself. No one puts their name out there (especially, in my case, where the length and unpronounceable foreign nature of one's name makes it a perfect target for mockery) in bold declarations and television scripts without hoping for fame and recognition.

The funny thing about name recognition is that it follows you to the good shows just as much as it does when you go to work on shows that suck. Even if that suckage is by no means a fault of your own.

Finally, it is absolutely possible that the reason I was

so hurt by Gharlane's constant sniping is that -- during all those years -- I never hopped back on the web and tried to give as good as I got.

A great man -- either Sun-Tzu or James T. Kirk -- once admonished his students never to march into battle unless victory was already assured. Rec.arts.sf (TV/written and otherwise) was Gharlane's citadel, built over years, decades even. He had fans, he had detractors, but he reigned supreme in a way that is probably impossible in today's internet, and for anyone without Gharlane's long history with the medium. If there is something I know -- and this is one of a very small number of sports analogies with which I am actually comfortable -- it is to never underestimate someone else's home court advantage.

After the whole *seaQuest/USA Today* incident, I was admonished by my bosses to stay the hell away from the internet, pretty please on pain of castration with a rusty spoon. Since I went from being a low-level network executive to being a low-level writer, I figured (and was often told in no uncertain -- and sometimes shockingly explicit -- terms) that it was better to leave the commenting on the state of networks and shows to those who actually run networks and shows.

So I took the advice of my superiors and lay low for the better part of a decade. The internet grew, I (hopefully) became a more practiced writer and producer -- though I still don't wield the kind of influence with which Gharlane credited me early in my career.

As big and wonderful as the web is, I found that it can be its own all-encompassing virtual world, and that I could just as easily prosper in any number of other worlds of my own -- or other people's -- making without ever again hearing the name "Gharlane of Eddore."

But, of course, I never shook the habit of self-Googling (or self-Alta-Vista-ing/Deja-Newsing, for those of you who remember the good ole days) every time I got on a new show... knowing that Gharlane's next missive would be there in all of its curmudgeonly glory as soon as my writing credit appeared on the screen.

Over the years, there was a lot of speculation as to Gharlane's true identity.

Was he Harlan Ellison (of course not -- the only keyboard Ellison ever touches is his trusty Smith Corona Selectric typewriter)?

Was he Locke to J. Michael Straczynski's Demosthenes?

David Gerrold on a bad day? A succession of REALLY bad days?

Or was he merely a highly educated -- and extremely pedantic -- polyglot/redhead worshipper working in IT at a State University Computer Science Department somewhere in Northern California?

What mattered more: who the man was, or the opinions he voiced on the internet?

In the summer of 2001, it stopped.

In its own chaotic way, the internet soon sorted it all out. Gharlane had indeed succumbed at a young age (he was in his '50s). His true identity was eventually revealed. The usual suspects who despised the man came out to grind their axes one last time. Gharlane's death and his influence on the Stone-Age of the World Wide Web was even reported in a few newspapers around the world.

Those who knew Gharlane personally tried to respect his well-cultivated anonymity while characterizing him as a decent man who treated his friends with kindness and generosity, worked hard, made a fair wage, and probably had the requisite number of foibles and peccadilloes every person accrues during the course of a lifetime. We should all be so well-remembered when we go.

When I read the news I felt a strange desolation.

For me, Gharlane's death brought to a conclusive end a time when I saw the web as mad, bad and dangerous to know. In the early to mid-90s, the internet was a frontier town underestimated by television producers, overestimated by its denizens, misunderstood by corporate executives, and likely to cause no end of trouble.

I suppose it's still that in a lot of ways -- but I would not have believed you if you had told me six years ago that I would be cultivating friendships with fans and expressing myself over the internet the way I do today.

One of my best friends frequently poses the question "If Batman died would The Joker truly be happy?"

While I don't think that is an entirely accurate depiction of my "relationship" with Gharlane of Eddore -- after all, we never met and never engaged in the war of words in either the real or virtual world, so what was it anyway? -- it does raise an interesting point. Whatever the man may have said about me, I certainly wasn't about to take glee or relief in his demise -- but I also had no real-life touchstone from which to base my feelings about his death.

Since Gharlane didn't know me, I can only assume I was a convenient fiction upon which he could easily project his hatred of supercilious young network executives who overstep their bounds, writers he felt unworthy of the vast audience automatically afforded them by the ubiquity of television (as opposed to hard, literary SF), and of crappy genre shows in general.

Truly, I felt sad and more than a little bit void. Not just for the death of another person, but because my own personal nemesis was gone -- and what kind of great protagonist can you be in the book of your life without at least one undefeatable adversary?

And, as I cruise through my thirty-fifth year and consider the state of the world around me, I desperately wish that Gharlane of Eddore were the only undefeatable adversary in my life.

THE THING I CAN'T SHAKE

Originally published February 27th and 28th, 2005, on Livejournal.

PART ONE

What constitutes a turning point? One of the most significant ones in my life came during my freshman year of college.

My two most important friends at the time were my roommate Jon and his friend Jonathan. They were "the Jons" as it were, and I -- being a year behind and significantly less worldly and socially adjusted -- made for a good mascot/little brother/whipping boy.

Jon was a complicated, mercurial sort -- prone to wild fits of inspiration and energy: an audacious firebrand who leapt face first where angels fear to tread. Jonathan was a silver-tongued charmer with enough native charisma to power a city.

The day I met Jonathan, I came home to find him sitting in our dining nook with Jon: they were having a chili pepper-eating contest, and chasing down the burn with vodka. Somewhere in the form and substance of that particularly masochistic competition is a metaphor for the common ground that formed the axis of their friendship, and the way they lived their lives.

More often than not, I would stumble home from

what I thought to have been a downright scandalous late night of movie viewing and hanging out at the campus coffeehouse only to have the Jons storm the apartment and order me to pack a suit and tie. Soon -- whether I wanted or not -- I would be on the road to Atlantic City, lying about my age to enter a casino, smoking cigars, drinking brandy from a snifter and looking fabulous.

As one might imagine would be the case with such diametrically opposed personalities -- they fought on more than one occasion.

And so, one mid-afternoon, as I entered the one-room, L-shaped university apartment I shared with Jon and hit the answering machine (something I did frequently, even when I had been in the room all day without hearing a ring), I found a turning point.

There was one message on the machine. From Jonathan to Jon:

"I don't like it when we fight like this, please give me a call so we can talk about it."

So how does eavesdropping on a private message constitute a turning point?

I had little experience with apologies. It wasn't an activity that seemed natural. Most teenage boys simply grunt their way through the inarticulate rituals of their lives without any thought. Sensitive and artistic as I may have been as a young man, I was as much a product of the environment as the next guy.

Not Jonathan. Conciliation was in his bones. Not weakness, mind you, but a natural ease with himself that, among other things, made it possible for him to casually extend a declaration of friendship and affection without that crippling, rapid-onset brainlock most men do not overcome until much later in life.

So that answering machine message was a revelation. Here was a young man who was everything a man any age would like to be: charming, sophisticated, intelligent, smooth... and at the root of all those qualities was an emotional wisdom that -- in what seemed completely counter-intuitive to a naive young mind raised on TV shows and action films -- translated into strength of character.

This wasn't an isolated event. The longer I got to know Jonathan, the more stunned I was by his often flagrant displays of decency and humanity. Had he not been such a likable person, one might have accused him of being a show-off.

That's not to say the man never made mistakes -- he had the same capacity for it as the rest of us -- but there was seldom a time when Jonathan's willingness and ability to take responsibility for his actions and broker a peace were not greater than any injury he might have caused.

And he was a good and giving friend.

We spent a huge amount of time driving around the country in his decrepit Buick Riviera. One time during my freshman year, we made a 36 hour round-trip trek to my hometown in the thick of a winter snowstorm because I felt homesick and, for some reason, the sum and substance of my mental health depended on my watching a musical at my old high school and attending the cast party afterward.

As you might expect, all the parties involved did a lot of eventful growing up in the years that followed. We all stayed friends, fell out, made up, and created lives for ourselves.

Jonathan cut a particularly impressive trajectory through life. It wasn't just that by the time he was a junior in college he had been asked by a financial giant to spend a semester working (among grown-ups no less!) in anticipation of an eventual permanent position -- or that by the time he was 32, he was named Managing Director of a world-leading venture capital company -- a lot of people achieve massive material success at a young age...

Many of them do it by being total bastards.

Not Jonathan. He rarely lost his temper or gave in to depression, despair or aggression -- even in the face of the painful growth everyone endures as they transition into adulthood.

In addition to his meteoric professional career, Jonathan sucked the marrow out of life and made the most of every moment -- he met and married a wonderful woman every bit his equal, had two beautiful children, fronted an affable cover band that played clubs in his hometown, painted (quite a feat for someone color-blind), and hosted amazing parties full of friendship and warmth -- most of which would end with his picking up a guitar and leading the last of the guests in song.

And unlike most of the people who pick up a guitar in a party (let's face it, there's a reason the funniest part of *Animal House* involves John Belushi smashing someone's guitar at a party), he came across as an unassuming host breaking out yet another diversion.

The song I remember him most frequently playing was Pink Floyd's "Wish You Were Here."

I remember Jonathan as a prince of the city. The kind of guy who -- even at a young age -- could stride into Peter Luger's steakhouse and receive hugs from the grumpy, inscrutable, pot-bellied old-timers who wait tables in that venerable New York establishment. Being Jonathan's friend was like taking a ride in a Duesenberg with the Rat

Pack -- only instead of Nelson Riddle, you would hear James Taylor playing on the radio...

As I write these lines, I ask myself: why is it so important for the living to canonize the dead?

I can't shake the feeling that we do it because it elevates us. Surely, if angels and heroes saw fit to seek out our company, then there must be something angelic and heroic about ourselves to make us worthy.

I should be so mercenary. It would make the loss that much more bearable.

On the last week of August, 2001, Jonathan phoned me. We had not seen each other in about six months, and hadn't talked in three or four. Even the best friendships suffer such lapses -- Jonathan had a globe-trotting, world-leading job and two children, and I had been steadily working in television and was a Producer on a series, but when the line connected, we were back in college:

"Javi, baby! We are brothers!"

Jonathan had a strange penchant for mixing Rat Pack lingo with his favorite Sean Connery line from *Highlander*.

We talked for a good 30 minutes. Jonathan had bought a Porsche after years of commuting to the city by train and felt the need to let me know -- in a very sheepish tone of voice, before anyone else told me -- so I could make all the requisite "early onset mid-life crisis" jokes with a minimum of obstruction.

Jonathan also gave me his office number yet again (I have a bad habit of never keeping anyone's number for too long), which I wrote on a sticky-note and posted it on my document stand. We then made plans for a trip to Las Vegas with Jon and a few other friends from college, and agreed to talk again in September to finalize the details of the trip.

Jonathan was murdered on September 11.

I won't get into the details of where I was when I heard about the attacks or the like. The world is awash with such stories.

Like everybody else, I spent the day on the phone and in front of the television. By the time night fell in Los Angeles, I was so worn that I popped a DVD of *Koyaanisqatsi* into the player and let it repeat for the rest of the night. I craved abstraction after an entire day of watching the American media straining to put narrative on the incomprehensible.

Not once did it occur to me that my friend -- whom I had been reminded less than two weeks before worked in the 105th floor of the World Trade Center -- was involved.

Why?

Maybe I had forgotten Jonathan's specific place of work. It's not unusual for me. I can quote verbatim from a toy commercial I saw when I was two, but, as of this writing, I've left my car keys in my office and had to walk back from the parking structure to get them for seven days straight.

More importantly, the very idea of Jonathan dying was beyond the scope of my comprehension.

Seriously. I don't clutch my head in disbelief at the unthinkable -- even when I can't understand it -- the world can be a cruel place, and while I do my best to be an optimist, the human capacity for destruction seldom catches me by surprise...

But no way Jonathan could be rubbed out.

Absolutely not.

Surely he was out there in his brand-new Porsche, flying through the freeways on some ill-advised road trip, blaring a Sinatra song with a big smile on his face.

Jonathan was larger than life -- there was no way I could fathom him being soiled by so terrible a display of the ugly side of the human soul.

And so I went through 9/11 experiencing many of the same emotions everybody did but not once thinking about Jonathan. The next day I went to my office, sat at my desk, and saw his office number scrawled on a sticky note on my document stand.

It was an Alfred Hitchcock-*Vertigo*-dolly-counterzoom moment. I was no longer a spectator; tragedy had just shown up at my door.

Stupidly, I dialed Jonathan's office number. I've always been that big a dolt. How someone as cool as Jonathan ever chose to befriend me is beyond my understanding.

Then I called his home. His father answered the phone. And I knew. Why else would Jonathan's father be at his house at noon on a weekday?

Six days later I flew to New York for Jonathan's funeral. Over 500 people attended. One of them sat next to me after the eulogies were said, and wearily mentioned he had 30 other funerals to attend that day.

I flew back to Los Angeles as soon as humanly possible.

In spite of it being Jonathan's base of operations, I have never liked New York City, and even before 9/11, I was always immune to its cosmopolitan charms. I never could shake my dread of that particular metropolis -- and believe me, coming from someone who suffers Los Angeles's many drawbacks because it is a geographical career necessity, that is a hell of an indictment.

On the night before Jonathan's funeral, I had dinner at the home of a mutual friend across the river from the World Trade Center. The ashes, dust, and smoke still hung in the air, backlit by the city: forming a nimbus that loomed over everything like a ghost -- a massive funeral pyre.

I have only been back to New York once since then and refused to visit Ground Zero. I found it morbid -- no, ghoulish -- that anybody would want to "visit" Ground Zero. Stranger still was the bizarre sense of envy I often got from people who had no personal connection to the tragedy.

I want to feign shock and claim that I don't understand the psychology behind that kind of thinking -- but, as a professional producer of televised narrative, I would be disingenuous. I understand it all to well.

9/11 was a televised spectacular -- and a lot of people would have killed to have a story to tell -- to have a part of the great tragic and heroic American narrative woven by the television networks with all of their myth-making prowess.

I do not want to imagine the hell the next few months must have been for Jonathan's family. His wife was widowed, his two children -- daughter still a babe in arms -- were orphaned, and his parents had to bury a son... and in spite of everyone's effort to move on, almost a year went by before Jonathan's remains were found and identified.

I grieve to this day.

That doesn't mean I haven't come to terms with the blunt-force brutality that led to Jonathan's death. Life goes on in spite of the awful truth that this beautiful man simply does not exist anymore -- we are forced to continue whether we like it or not -- and at the very least I have the memory and example of how Jonathan lived his life to ameliorate the pain of how that life was ended.

But there is something else that gnaws at me.

Jonathan left a legacy -- everyone who knew him

was deeply affected by the joy with which he lived. He taught me one of the most valuable life lessons I have ever learned. His work on this planet may not have been done, but no doubt he earned his way into heaven.

Which demands that I continually ask myself the question that is at the root of my current malaise: how are we, as Americans, going to be remembered after September 11?

Because I don't see us as a nation earning our way into heaven any time soon.

PART TWO

The thing I can't shake is a looming dread over the path our country has taken -- a pervasive sense of depression and rage that is visited upon me with every foreign policy announcement and every news report of the motion of the American war machine.

Before you roll your eyes and say "Oh dear lord, here's another overeducated, overfed, overpaid, privileged Hollywood liberal lecturing us about the evil ways of our Republican government..."

Let me make one thing clear. This is not intended as a partisan screed. Anybody who reads this journal knows where I stand politically, but -- make no mistake -- I would be writing these same words were a Democrat in the Oval Office.

This is not about political alignment -- it's about morality and ethics.

After September 11, the President sought to answer the question "Why do they hate us?"

Frankly, I don't know why he sought to answer this question. Nor do I know if many people over the age of ten actually asked themselves the question. The President -- who clearly sees himself as a father figure to the country -- must see all of us as infants, because that is the way he chose to frame the popular discourse in the time following 9/11.

I have an answer to which I subscribe. "They" hate us for decades of selfish, short-sighted and destructive foreign policy -- foisted by Republicans and Democrats alike -- designed to keep us in cheap foreign oil.

Don't believe that one? Try this one: they hate us for cozying up to oppressive regimes led by the likes of Saddam Hussein, Mohammed Reza Pahlevi, the Taliban and the House of Saud because -- while we advertise ourselves as exporters of Democracy -- some animals are just more equal than others.

Don't like that one? Here's another one: they hate us because they hate freedom.

I like it...

Apparently so do a lot of other people, because "They hate freedom" is the reason our armies are spread so thin and taking casualties around the world as we speak.

"They hate freedom" is the reason we described the so-called Axis of Evil and rattle our saber for more conflict even though our troops are currently bolting refrigerator doors to the sides of their Humvees because the people in charge of defense logistics never imagined that we would engage in so widespread and long-lasting a conflict.

"They hate freedom" is the reason we have taken it upon ourselves go at it alone and disarm the bad guys.

As a professional writer -- someone who struggles daily to harness the power of words to make people believe in a reality of my own making -- I envy the author of "they hate freedom."

It is the most elegantly succinct piece of fiction I have ever known. Simple to the point of art. Easily grasped by anyone who reads it, "They hate freedom" demands no understanding of history or politics to make itself understood. It tells the word that we are on the side of good and anyone who opposes us is in the side of evil. "They hate freedom" -- not us, they -- and "they" could be anybody who isn't us.

Just keep repeating it to yourself. It feels great. Better than any food, drug or medicine I have ever ingested. It is the ultimate justification; a warm blanket of comfort deafening the cries of the world outside.

And if you don't believe it, maybe you hate freedom too. And what could be sicker -- more warped, more demented and inhuman -- than hating freedom?

Here's another statement that is also very much in vogue in our popular culture -- "what would Jesus do?"

I like this statement because I am a Christian. I love God and subscribe, without shame or fear or guilt, to the truth of Jesus Christ as God made flesh -- sent to earth to provide a vivid, concrete and lasting example of the values to which we humans should aspire.

That much said, I am not a particularly good Christian. I have a lot of difficulty attending Mass on a regular basis, and while I pray consistently and try to live according to a Christian ethic, I do not know scripture to the extent that I should, and often find myself in willing exile from the Episcopal church I attend.

The reasons why are complex -- and I won't try to sell you (as I did myself for a long time) on the idea that "I practice my faith in private," because I am of the belief that one needs to be in the company of others more spiritually advanced than one's self in order to truly grow and learn.

Every athlete needs a coach, the same applies to the spiritual realm.

Bottom line: I am writing this with a copy of *The Bible for Dummies* in one hand and openly defying Jesus' own admonition against those "who practice their righteousness before others in order to be noticed by them."

The great thing about Jesus Christ is that he left very little up for interpretation. "Turn the other cheek," "blessed are the peacemakers" and "do unto others as you would have them do unto you" are statements of adamantine simplicity. Could one find shading and nuance? Sure, but, at their core, these statements are as simple and easily understood as "They hate freedom," and they have the added benefit of constituting a system of ethics as opposed to a rationalization for any behavior we see fit.

Of course, you could ask me why I don't believe in the death penalty, and I could give you two answers. One of them is the flawed, human one that betrays a dark soul that doesn't entirely frown on the idea of vengeance -- lifetime imprisonment in a life-crushing hellhole where the prisoner is in constant danger of being anally raped is a fate worse than death. The other is infinitely simpler: "Which part of 'Thou shall not kill' didn't you get?"

The point: I am a hypocrite -- which, according to *The Bible for Dummies* comes from an archaic term for actors in a play -- doing it for spectacle instead of for internal reasons of truth-seeking or spiritual growth.

Our President, however, is a veteran of one of the most vigorous Christian fellowships in our country -- the Midland Community Bible Study in Texas -- and he claims Jesus Christ as the most important and influential person in his life. In so many words -- in issues of both foreign and domestic policy -- he has made Christianity one of the pillars of his agenda and ideological design for his stewardship of the United States.

Which raises the inevitable question -- why is the United States of America behaving in such an unchristian way?

The week after September 11, I sat alone in a hotel room in New York City following Jonathan's funeral. It was freezing in the room -- I always turn the AC on full blast when I stay in a hotel (what can I say? I like cold, dry environments) and I was weighing whether or not to numb the pain of the last week with scotch and Spectravision.

That was the night that our President gave the "Axis of Evil" speech.

It was in the course of that speech that I first felt the hard, darkening dread that fills me to this day. The culmination of my every dyspeptic, paranoid Orwellian speculation: the moment the United States crossed through the looking glass.

Before that day, our President had been a joke to me -- a slam-dunk one-termer to be endured with a stiff upper lip... hopefully soon to be consigned to the dustbin of history as a "caretaker" President.

After that day he became a nightmare.

That night, the President took it upon himself to declare his office as judge, jury and executioner by naming other nations as evil and threatening quasi-divine retribution.

Now, last I checked, that was God's job... but let's humor the guy -- he is, after all, the President.

My impression is that taking it upon one's self to make the judgment call of who is good and evil and mete out punishment implies moral superiority. So where has our moral superiority taken us in the past four years?

To me, 9/11 was the ultimate opportunity for the United States to take the high road -- to prove itself the most evolved and sophisticated nation in the world. How might we have accomplished that?

We could have truly declared war on the aggressors, rallied the nations of the world into a cohesive alliance based on the sharing of intelligence and military assets and made the world a truly inhospitable place for terrorists. Remember -- this was a time when *Le Monde*, arguably France's newspaper of record, printed the statement "We are all Americans."

The world was ready to be led into a historical coalition now that its last remaining superpower had fallen victim to something almost every other nation had already experienced on some scale. Together, we could have brought Osama Bin Laden to justice. Together we could have sent a strong clear message to the aggressors -- that the rest of the world had embraced an evolutionary unity averse to the use of terror for political ends.

And while I am describing what is clearly a crackpot, bleeding-heart liberal dream, let me make another suggestion...

We could have taken what recovering alcoholics refer to as "a fearless moral inventory." We could have evaluated the historical faults of our foreign policy in the Middle East and embarked on a new course of diplomatic action based on conciliation and understanding. We could have made a true effort to understand "why do they hate us?" and followed it with an aggressive initiative to win the support of the very same people who are now plotting to murder us.

In short, we could have turned the other cheek on an

unprecedented global scale.

For those of you who still think the expression means "let them hit you again and again until you die," here's some news: it means "shame the aggressor into complicity."

Would it have been difficult? You bet. Nigh-impossible and maybe even doomed to failure. It would have been a task whose complexity would have been equal to the Space Race, the Manhattan Project, and the Cuban Missile Crisis rolled into one. Worth trying? More than anything else -- and, in failure, the result might have still been significantly better than the world in which we presently find ourselves.

I don't have to tell you how we actually responded. We will be reaping the fruits of it for generations to come in terms of social paranoia, decimation of civil rights, and, most importantly, the loss of our political and economic capital with the rest of the world.

The list of people who "hate freedom" just keeps growing, even though I can't think -- not even for a moment -- of what it could possibly be that makes hating freedom so attractive.

Then again, I may hate freedom myself.

Why else would I even dare to suggest that our post-9/11 foreign policy and subsequent adventures in Iraq have been -- to use a highly technical military term -- a Mongolian clusterfuck?

The Bible -- our President's self-proclaimed handbook for personal ethics -- says, "Thou shalt not bear false witness," and yet we know that the theoretical foundation for our war on Iraq was flawed, misrepresented and, ultimately, fraudulent. We know that very high level people in our government were fully aware of the torture and abuses going on in our military prisons and shunted off their responsibility to the lower ranks. We know many things -- and they all point out to the kind of outrage that led Jesus to kick the moneychangers out of the temple.

Jesus said, "Blessed are the peacemakers" and yet we wage aggressive war on trumped-up charges against an opponent that had no connection to the 9/11 attacks. In doing so, we have helped create an insurgency that will eventually find its way to our homes, schools and places of business and recreation. We have made the world a more dangerous, more hateful, more paranoid place.

Jesus told the parable of the good Samaritan specifically because Samaritans were reviled at the time as weirdos with an unpalatable culture and religion. They were the great, frightening unwashed that could just not be trusted. With this parable, Jesus made a simple point against racial prejudice... and yet our government persists in pursuing a foreign policy that has done little more than foment hatred and social injustice against Muslims here and abroad.

Jesus said, "Blessed are the merciful, for they shall receive mercy," but our God-fearing President's foreign policy bears a greater resemblance to the slightly better-known axiom "don't mess with Texas."

As far as I can see, our government seems concerned with creating a fertile ground for only one of Jesus' teachings: "Blessed are those who mourn, for they shall be comforted."

But let's say you just aren't into all of this Jesus mumbo-jumbo. Hey -- I can respect that -- let's go to someone who ought to know what he is talking about...

Robert McNamara was chief architect of the Vietnam War: a war characterized by Lyndon Johnson (in what should be very familiar language) as a struggle "against tyranny and aggression." To this day, McNamara is reviled by many as a warmonger and demagogue, he is a man whose very name makes most of the baby-boomer liberals in my acquaintance snarl with anger and contempt...

But during the interviews that made up Errol Morris's film *The Fog of War*, McNamara makes the statement that:

> *"We are the most powerful nation in the world -- economically, politically, and militarily -- and we are likely to remain so for decades ahead. But we are not omniscient. If we cannot persuade other nations with similar interests and similar values of the merits of our proposed use of that power, we should not proceed unilaterally."*

Some argue that, to this day, the ruthless application of military force has solved more problems worldwide than any other manifestation of diplomacy. It's probably true.

But it doesn't mean there isn't a better way.

If we have the power to rain destruction on any nation of our choosing, then doesn't the man most directly responsible for wielding that power owe it to the world -- especially when he invokes Jesus Christ as his Lord, Savior, and Role Model -- to use that power wisely (and if the required wisdom is just not present, to at least try to apply the values taught by Jesus Christ)?

Let's face it, Jesus Christ -- being the human manifestation of The Almighty -- could have blinked and turned us all into hermit crabs. However, to the extent that one can impose values of human morality on an omniscient, infinitely powerful being, he did not: because

Jesus Christ's mission on earth was not -- as many believe -- to drug the downtrodden into acceptance of their sad lot in this life with promises of a better world to come. It was to serve warning to the powerful that their privilege did not constitute a blank check for cruelty.

Jesus Christ was a revolutionary who spoke to power the truth that there is an evolutionary way to wield the political and military weapons of man with humility, tolerance and dignity.

I keep hearing that our President's rival lost the election because he failed to articulate a coherent alternate vision of America.

While I believe that America should be a secular state, I also believe that, since our President used Jesus Christ to set the table, his adversaries should have been ready to meet him in that arena -- ironically, the place where his footing is weakest -- and point out the ways, which are legion, in which the President has failed to honor his own stated commitment to the Christian ethic. That might have been the beginning of a vision of an America willing to take responsibility for its actions and confront its mistakes with honesty and strength of character.

Frankly, there are worse things -- whether you are a religious person or not -- than to advocate a foreign policy based on the hard work of coalition-building, conciliation, peace seeking, and tolerance: none of which, by the way, cancel out the necessity or possibility of bringing the aggressors to justice or providing for our own internal security. We should not be above kicking the moneychangers out of the temple on occasion.

Our present government is a profoundly hypocritical concern pursuing -- in the name of morality and Christian values -- a destructive, soul-poisoning set of foreign and domestic policy goals that point to an increasingly bleak future.

Our government excels at performing the intellectual contortions necessary to interpret a passage from Leviticus as an indictment of gay marriage -- or pushing a so-called "decency bill" that would punish someone for saying "fuck" on the air with the kind of severity reserved for those who illegally test pesticides on human subjects -- but cannot bring itself to translate the simplest of beatitudes delivered by Jesus on the Mount into a practical modern political reality.

I take our government's offenses personally -- not only because of my religious convictions -- but because the friend I lost on 9/11 was one of the greatest conciliators I ever knew. He wasn't a Christian, and I have no idea about his political slant -- but he was, to me, an example of a life lived with a surfeit of common human decency.

And although the United States is full of individuals who exhibit nothing but common human decency, our government has turned our country -- in the eyes of many who live here and abroad -- into a faceless war machine bent on stomping out dissent no matter what the cost.

Is this our legacy?

I don't know. Unlike our President, I don't have a direct line to God.

THE RIGHT TO NOT BEAR ARMS

Originally published on social media on January 26, 2013, in apropos of David Mamet's essay "Gun Laws and the Fools of Chelm" in that week's issue of Newsweek.

My death is not only inevitable, it is also imminent. No, I have neither been diagnosed with a lethal ailment and given minutes to live, nor am I contemplating suicide once I am done putting this down. I merely mean that my life is a mere flash in the two million or so years in which humanity has walked the earth.

Seen in the perspective of that time frame, the end of my life is, in fact, coming very soon -- whenever in my life it may choose to arrive. I might as well accept it.

I think about that whenever the topic of gun control comes up... especially when a Czar of American Letters™ like David Mamet picks up the quill to write a barn-burning opinion piece (like that on the cover of this week's *Newsweek*) in which he insists that the right to bear arms is an essential component to society; both in that it insures protection against the corrupt depredations of an increasingly intrusive government, as well as in that it is an essential prophylactic against incivility. In Mamet's philosophy, no one dares to be an aggressor in a society in which every man, woman, and child is given the inalienable right to carry guns.

In short: mutually assured destruction is the best insurance of our right to life. In the macro: should the government overstep, an armed populace will rise to pull it down. In the micro: if you kill, you will be killed.

Mamet's argument is lucid, consistent, and takes its cues from his -- and many other intelligent people's -- interpretation of the frame of reference and aims of the Founding Fathers. It does not surprise me that many whom I consider to be level-headed intellects feel as Mamet does: that an individual is the best and only person to decide how to defend themselves, and that, in this world, an individual can only properly accomplish that goal in possession of a firearm.

Still...reading Mamet's piece, I could not help but be struck by the preening, hypermasculine worship of conflict implicit in his every sentence. The bedrock conviction that the natural state of humanity is ideological crisis which will erupt into violence at any moment is implicit in his thesis, as well as his beliefs about the role of government, and the individual, in society.

I suppose this should not come as a surprise from Mamet. His work, from the sacred *Glengarry Glen Ross*, to the profane -- his martial arts film *Redbelt* and his television series *The Unit* -- range from what is essentially a Valentine to the poetry of emotional abuse to sustained explorations of the ability to enforce one's mark in combat against aggressors in a world that is viciously opposed to mutual understanding.

To live in the world expressed by Mamet -- and, to some degree, to live in the world of most who believe in the socially sanctioned ability to take a life when necessary -- is to live in (to borrow and recontextualize a phrase from Carl Sagan) a "demon-haunted world." It is a prison:

a maze in which predators lurk behind every corner and meanness of the soul is either prime motivator or inevitable outcome.

The Founding Fathers must have believed in this world, being as they flagged the right to bear arms in a language as carefully considered as the right to life, liberty, and the pursuit of happiness... and, again, it makes situational sense: they had been oppressed by a totalitarian monarchy and were surrounded by natives who were -- understandably -- hostile to their genocidal designs on their ancestral homeland.

All of which raises the more important question: when does humanity evolve from the right to bear arms to the right not to?

The study of violence in television -- a topic concomitant with issues relating to guns -- has yielded a phrase which has bounced in my head since I first encountered it: "mean world syndrome." The concept is simple: the depiction of violence in popular culture may or may not incite actual violence, but it almost certainly creates the indelible -- and vastly exaggerated -- impression in viewers that the world is a nasty, brutish place in which violence is not only an acceptable means by which to resolve conflict, but also a complete inevitability.

The belief in a mean world may be profitable for gun manufacturers, but I believe it is a cancer of the soul and an impediment to evolution.

Evolution is a difficult proposition, just as "Thou shalt not kill" is a difficult admonition to follow -- especially when others want what you have and have no moral barriers to its acquisition. It is harder to reason than to kill, it is harder to compromise than to kill, it is harder to exercise empathy than to kill, it is harder to persuade, to forgive, to make a fearless moral inventory of our own wrongs, and to leave others to do the same and see the error of their own ways, than to kill.

It is -- admittedly -- harder to accomplish pretty much anything without the threat of a reckoning than it is to swing a big stick; and yet, over and over, since the evolution of consciousness, the prohibition of murder continues to be the central tenet of human spiritual and ethical growth. I believe this to be an evolutionary adaptation -- a call across the eons telling us that the next step in our development as a species is collaboration and nonviolence.

In spiritual terms, the hard simplicity of the statement "Thou shalt not kill" makes its challenge frighteningly clear. It does not say, "Thou shalt not kill save for cases of home invasion" or "Thou shalt not kill except for when your way of life is being threatened by a formerly democratic government that has really gotten way too autocratic for its britches" and it sure as shekels doesn't say, "Thou shalt not kill save for in the case of an organized state militia."

For all the embellishments that human beings put in their spiritual traditions -- usually designed to tell others how to live their lives in stultifying, homogeneous obedience and keep out undesirables -- it is surprising how often the prohibition of murder shows up. The seeds of virtue are programmed to survive the death of the individual: "Thou shalt not kill" -- in all of its forms, across secular and spiritual thought -- keeps outliving people, democracies and dictatorships.

That is evolution at work.

Evolution is difficult and inconvenient to expediency. However, as I have been blessed with the luxury of living in what is -- arguably -- a democracy in which my participation is still allowed, of the opportunity to make a living in my chosen field, of a surfeit of creature comforts and technological expediency, of a preponderance of like-minded individuals who share my faith in God and my reliance on a number of societal systems designed to further my way of life -- usually at the expense of others -- I believe that I have a duty to make my life difficult in, at the very least, some minuscule but relevant way.

Chris Hedges famously titled one of his books *War Is a Force That Gives Us Meaning*. His argument is that both the perception and reality of never-ending battle instills in human beings a sense of purpose. As long as there is someone or something to oppose, the soul is filled with the comforting tonic of simplicity: don't worry about empathy, reason, the truth that all humans are genetically identical, or the underlying unity of world religion and ethics, shoot to kill. Indulge your need for violent conquest and all the fuss and muss of worldly life becomes a distant memory. There's an addictive satisfaction and perverse joy in that clarity.

The bearing of arms, and the perception of it as a right is -- to me -- a vestige of a primal addiction to violence, and the anodyne ease of a life led in Manichean opposition: an expression of the spirit-destroying contradiction that to be alive and free is to be on constant alert for coming war. To be armed is to never lose sight of the possibility that at any time we may be called upon to reassert our triumphant masculinity through the application of lethal force.

I believe that finding a way of life that does not automatically see in strangers the threat of extinction -- that takes kindness, tolerance and collaboration as the first assumption of human coexistence -- is both a Christian and Darwinian ideal: a natural continuation of the rise of consciousness. I refuse to be a walking deterrent -- just as I refuse to be a talking inciter -- of violence.

I believe that there is an evolutionary imperative -- expressed across a majority of spiritual and secular traditions -- for the prohibition of murder under any circumstance. I aspire to live in a society where fear of the other is not understood as the baseline, and feel duty-bound to that aspiration because the accident of my birth in the wealthiest and freest nation on the planet affords me the privilege to strive for that ideal.

I believe that the responsibility that accompanies the largely unearned rewards of my privilege -- and that of almost every other American -- is the exploration of a way of life in which that bounty is no longer earned through violence or exploitation.

I have made peace with the inevitability of my own death. Statistically, the greatest likelihood is that the end of my life will come as a result of heart disease brought about by the excessive consumption of processed foods.

Even in our gun-loving, violence-obsessed, perpetually-in-Defcon-1 United States of America, the possibility of my dying as a result of a violent incident involving firearms -- even one involving terrorists carrying firearms -- is lower than an automobile accident, plane crash, or lightning strike. So I will not carry a gun in expectation of the one-man war that my very way of life has already conspired to prevent.

I will use my freedom to employ words, actions, and ideas to convince others that to strap on a cold reminder of the ability to take life is not a freeing act, but a bondage to a way of life that must be stopped...

And if I'm shot by a terrorist, or a jackbooted foot-soldier of a totalitarian regime -- or even a common criminal?

Forgive them.

Or don't. I won't care. I'll be dead... and the life of my killers, and whatever they stood for that was so important that it required my extinction, will end just as quickly, cosmically speaking, as mine.

I refuse my right to bear arms because I prefer to advocate for my right not to.

I refuse my right to bear arms because I believe that to be the truest expression of the privilege for which so many have killed and died.

I refuse my right to bear arms because I believe that Gandhi, Einstein, Sagan, Jesus, Buddha -- and even Ayn Rand, whose words I'll quote as a credibility-destroying concession to a young adulthood misspent re-reading *Atlas Shrugged* -- agreed on one thing:

"Force and mind are opposites; morality ends where a gun begins."

WHAT FIVE YEARS OF ARGUING ABOUT POLITICS ON SOCIAL MEDIA HAS TAUGHT ME

Originally published on March 24, 2013, on various social media.

Submitted with apologies to George Orwell and Jonathan Heidt, whose book *The Righteous Mind* should be required reading -- and whose insights are most likely paraphrased below as I struggled to articulate my own.

> *"The war is not meant to be won, it is meant to be continuous. Hierarchical society is only possible on the basis of poverty and ignorance...in principle the war effort is always planned to keep society on the brink of starvation. The war is waged by the ruling group against its own subjects and its object is not the victory...but to keep the very structure of society intact."*
> -- **George Orwell, 1984**

> *"We also have the ability, under special circumstances, to...become like cells in a larger body, or like bees in a hive, working for the good of the group. These experiences*

are often among the most cherished of our
lives, although our hivishness can blind us
to other moral concerns. Our bee-like nature
facilitates altruism, heroism, war, and
genocide."
   -- Jonathan Heidt, *The Righteous Mind*

"There's no such thing as an American
anymore. No Hispanics, no Japanese, no
blacks, no whites, no nothing. It's just rich
people and poor people. The three of us are
all rich, so we're on the same side."
   -- dialogue from *Deep Cover,* screenplay by
   Michael Tolkin

S parring with friends and enemies on social networks over several years has taught me that our political ideologies, party affiliations, and tribal loyalties are a distraction. I now believe that the sole polarities in our world are power and poverty.

Power -- as embodied by wealth, celebrity, and influence -- seeks one goal: to extend its tenure. Poverty is the state power must foster in individuals to succeed. Poverty of intellect. Poverty of spirit. Poverty of means.

The United States may be the most materially wealthy nation in the world, but when the prosperity and privilege of its citizens is taken into account, it may also be the most intellectually and spiritually impoverished.

This is not a coincidence.

Freedom from poverty in a society where the tools of liberation are openly available doesn't demand armed revolt, open warfare, or even the threat of violence. Freedom only demands that we use something from which power cannot profit -- our individual intellect and compassion -- and do with it something from which no one can gain power: organize respectfully around temporary consensus.

Power wants individuals to believe that the enemy of freedom is the other. The liberal next door, the conservative in the other voting booth -- even abstract notions of "the individual" and "the collective" -- are soldiers to be demonized, marginalized, and ultimately defeated on an intimate level.

Power wants us to believe that to agree and take action, we must agree on everything. Power wants you to think that an individual who believes in one thing in which you do not is unfit to stand with you on another.

Power -- in collusion with the reptile brain bent on survival -- wants perennial conflict based on difference because opposition based on any consensus, however temporary, is lethal to power.

Power thrives on perpetuating within the individual psyche the idea of monolithic, conspiratorial opposition. This is not a monolithic conspiracy but a freely obtainable mechanism to increase poverty.

From the slogan that insists on the superiority of users of one product over those of another identical commodity, to the religious sect that insists its primacy even over who study the same scripture, and the political parties who divide those whose common goals by far outnumber their differences, power uses the Darwinian impulse to retard the evolutionary need.

Power needs the individual to believe that survival depends on obliterating the competition. Power requires individuals to believe that resources are limited, the crisis is at hand, and the only way to survive is by increasing the poverty of another. Power seeks to destroy the individual, preferably by getting other individuals to do the work for them.

Power's main weapon against the individual is the illusion that by aligning with power, the individual will possess power. Power seduces with aspirational ideals: this party represents prosperity, that product represents intellectual superiority, this religion represents spiritual supremacy.

Power increases poverty of diversity with promises of individual dominion but never addresses the contradiction that power is reserved for an elite few. The seduced mind assumes it is chosen.

We are victims of power, but the seduction of power prevents the individual from acceptance. Power obfuscates its influence by teaching as the idea that victimization equals weakness -- and weakness is a form of poverty. Power is desirable, poverty is not. An admission of poverty is a sign of personal failure, not systemic deprivation.

The individual sanctions the depredations of power through denial. Power has no use for the individual who recognizes that it casts leaders and foot soldiers into poverty with equal disdain. Power needs individuals to believe that they will be immune -- even though death is the ultimate end to all personal power.

The polarized, polarizing political climate of the United States in 2013 is part of a vast, unorganized, non-conspiratorial order that has evolved around the protection of power.

Corporations have the rights of individuals though their behavior would cause an individual to be jailed. Governments command carnage on easily disproved premises because individuals are too divided by the comfort of partisan conflict to evaluate facts on their merits and organize accordingly.

Power induces poverty of empathy: reducing individuals to abstractions and tragedy to statistics. The citizenry permits this because where politics are sport, someone must belong to the losing team, and consensus -- even short-term consensus around issues of pressing moral import -- has been marketed as moral weakness.

We thus forgive the crimes of ideological fellow-travelers as the necessary sacrifices of "the real world," identify the crimes of antagonists as proof of their moral failing, and ignore points of common benefit around which individuals can collude to undo the influence of power without compromising their integrity.

Conciliation, compromise -- and the ability to identify and achieve common goals in spite of difference -- are the only assets individuals can leverage to mitigate poverty.

An acceptance that an individual can only wield power temporarily -- that wealth is transitory, influence is fluid, and that the only benefit to having power is to freely prepare to hand over that power to as many others as possible -- is the only guarantee of an ongoing check on power.

No one can lead without falling prey to the corrupting influence of power who does not accept power with the concomitant understanding that the individual, while essential, has an expiration date. Power must be shared and many must be groomed to lead.

The individual and the collective must coexist -- though individual pride chafes at the notion of alliance with the other and collectives by nature demand homogeneity. Groups collude around individual visions, visions can only survive the transfer when given freely and with trust, the group can only survive if the individuals within preserve and act according to their own integrity.

As it is with the collective and the individual, so it goes with power and poverty. One causes the other. One needs the other. One can ameliorate the other. There are no pure forms of either and neither is going to disappear: not because of some ideal of perpetual war between good and evil, but because we are born into poverty, mature into insight and exit into the ultimate poverty of existence.

Poverty flourishes where individuals and collectives favor one over the other. The balance is where we must choose to live. Though our world is increasingly linked, power knows that these avenues of communication can easily be transformed into roadblocks. Power knows that to flourish unchecked it need not be totalitarian but merely distracting -- it is our work to see the distractions and settle for something more difficult than the comfort they provide.

FINDING THE NEXT LOST: WHAT IS AN "OPERATIONAL THEME" AND WHY DON'T I HAVE ONE?

Originally published online by Apex magazine, May 24, 2013.

O ne of the many perks afforded a journeyman writer/producer in television is receiving scripts for network television pilots as they are being made. It's like the best possible version of the *TV Guide* Fall Preview Issue I used to compulsively reread under the covers with a flashlight as a kid. Except that now I have the added thrill: if my agents do their job, if I am good in the interview, if a million other moving parts click in the correct order, I help the people who created these shows realize their vision.

This inside window into the totality of network development puts us journeyman television writers and producers in an interesting position to spot and track trends as they develop, fade, or mature. One trend that persists -- almost a decade after its inception -- is every broadcaster's ongoing quest to put on the air the next great serialized high-concept sci-fi show: to find the next *Lost*.

Of course, it seldom works.

My own modest contribution to the evolution of *Lost* --

and having worked on a number of shows with similar goals in the years since -- provides something of a vantage point from which to judge the success -- and failure -- of these attempts. More often than not, it boils down to the presence or absence of a crucial element I call "the operational theme."

In high school and college, most of us could pick a lofty word or idea and designate it the "theme" of a play or novel: "power," "alienation," "banality of evil," or (my personal favorite) "the shallowness of modern life." We could then write a coffee--and--Red-Bull-fueled paper, using choice quotes from the partially--skimmed bit of required reading, and have a pretty good shot at not winding up ashamed to show the report card to our parents in the morning. Sadly, for the professional television writers -- even the really astute ones -- this is neither enough to create something that will connect with an audience, nor will it survive the production goal of many seasons and possible syndication.

Television is a populist medium with little patience for intellectual phumphering. Hour-long drama is -- first and foremost -- about creating characters driven by internal forces that, melded to the right situation, can fuel every action, every line, every scene, and every plot for hundreds of successful episodes. This is the operational theme: a situational vector that cleanly delineates the potential variations of action in service of the protagonist's consistent emotional need. This is *crucial* to the success of a television pilot. It is crucial to the successful episodes to come. It is, indeed, what television pilots should see as the first order of business to establish. And yet, it is most often the part that's missing -- especially from the sci-fi shows.

In a procedural series, the operational theme of the

protagonist is usually pretty cut-and-dry. He or she is
-- sometimes quite literally -- dedicated to bringing about
law and order. The reason cops, doctors, and lawyers rule
-- and will probably always rule -- the airwaves in some
form or another is that their operational theme is baked
into their personality. It is a function of their job -- the
eradication of suffering and injustice at any cost -- and is
usually fused with personal obsession brought about by
past trauma.

If television is to be believed, the most dangerous thing
to be in the world is the spouse of a detective. Most of
them wind up dead at the hands of some psychopath who
remains uncatchable for the span of episodes it takes to
score a lucrative syndication deal for the series. Television
thrives on workaholic protagonists who sacrifice -- or have
sacrificed for them -- their personal relationships in favor
of protecting people like us -- the viewer!

As television has evolved to include more serialized,
heavily "mythologized" drama -- even in the stock genres
of crime, medicine, and the law -- the operational theme of
the protagonist must remain front and center for the series
to succeed. In *Breaking Bad*, Walter White's operational
theme -- "To save everything I love I must become
something everyone hates" -- creates an endless supply of
drama. Every situation Walter enters requires him to tell,
develop, and sustain a lie.

This brilliant operational theme requires every single
scene in the show to be front-loaded with deception and
subterfuge. It's a recipe for perfect ongoing drama that
allowed the show to slowly string out and develop its
more academic theme: the seduction of a good man by
the infinite charms of wealth, power, and his descent into
darkness. But make no mistake, academic is the right

word for those themes. It was the initial simplicity of Walter White's *operational* theme that consistently opened dramatic avenues episode after episode.

It doesn't end with Walter White. The current "golden era" of television is littered with very easily identifiable operational themes that burden their protagonists. Tony Soprano wants to remain a sadistic mobster even though his unconscious musters every weapon at its disposal to get him to turn away from his horrific life. Don Draper continually tries to keep up the idealized appearance of the successful mid-century man in the grey flannel suit as his inner demons plague him with the truth that his entire life is a lie. Doctor House wants to be left in peace to be a belligerent drug addict but is forced to put his basic instincts aside and perform the job of genius diagnostician.

Outside of TV, my favorite example of the perfect fusion of situation and character into operational theme is the film *Die Hard*. The entire narrative is an extended metaphor for marital therapy: a husband trying to earn back his estranged wife. The terrorists are the physical manifestation of the emotional barriers that keep John McClane from familial bliss. As with any person in couples counseling, McClane systematically loses his metaphorical armor as he fights to the point of exhaustion. He ends up shoeless and bloody, blubbering to his "therapist" about his love for his wife -- bleeding both thematically and practically.

The bathroom confession in *Die Hard* could have just easily been an episode of HBO's *In Treatment*: a man denuded through adversity of all the trappings of macho pride, forced to confront his raw emotional wounds.

It seems obvious, and, frankly, inevitable -- in the way that a Mark Rothko painting, or an Arne Jacobsen chair, appear inevitable -- that simple operational themes are the key to serialized success. And yet, by and large, most attempts at serialized, mythologized sci-fi fail to pull off this trick. Think of all the genre series that have attempted to capitalize on the serialized mystery / heavy-- mythology vogue triggered by *Lost*: *Flash Forward, Kingdom Hospital, Surface, The Event, Invasion, V, Threshold, Awake, Journeyman, Dollhouse, Persons Unknown, Terra Nova*, the American remake of *Life on Mars* -- the list goes on and on.

Most of the sci-fi shows we now regard as classics -- and the majority that are currently successful and truly long-running, like *Supernatural* -- are not *Lost* clones. Rather, they are straightforward procedural franchises with simple operational themes.

The brothers Winchester, Nick Burkhardt in *Grimm*, Mulder and Scully in *The X-Files* -- even *Buffy, the Vampire Slayer* -- are all basically cops: rolling into a new case week after week, interrogating suspects, finding lore that matches the methodology of the villains, confronting evildoers, serving justice, and moving on to the next week's transgressor. In the best of these series, an overarching theme buttresses the set-up: Mulder and Scully's dynamic was defined by opposing viewpoints which fueled every scene. In addition to being thrust into stories by their occupation every week, they always had a basic ideological conflict that spoke to their character.

Even the beloved crew of the Starship Enterprise are hyper-competent trouble-shooters placed into stories weekly by dint of external mission as opposed to internal need. In the best *Star Trek* series, this necessity was supported by an interesting character dynamic: Captain Kirk, Spock, and McCoy are a three-man representation of the ego, superego, and id. The drama of the series lied in watching these three archetypes integrate into a coherent solution to the planet-of-the-week's problem: McCoy would shout, "Dammit, man, we gotta do something!" Spock would reply that, "To do something would be illogical." Kirk would eventually say, "I have a plan."

Compare that infinitely fruitful character interaction with the first two seasons of *Star Trek: The Next Generation* -- a long and tedious stew of underdeveloped, under-thought characters kept afloat by the exigencies of a procedural franchise. On *Star Trek: The Next Generation*'s first two years there was always a potentially interesting issue with the planet-of-the-week. But it took almost two years for the characters to become anywhere as interesting as the show's premise.

(It's a miracle of the extant love of *Star Trek* in the core audience, or the innate intrigue of the show's premise, or the economics of first-run syndication in the late eighties -- or maybe some combination of the three -- that the show survived long enough for its characters to find their way into being fully-realized people who could carry a story like "The Inner Light," "Chains of Command," or "Tapestry.")

Had the writers merely dropped the original characters of *Star Trek: The Next Generation* on a desert island -- a place with no innate sense of mission -- the series would have surely collapsed.

Lost succeeded in telling a longitudinal story because it managed to create a central operational theme for every single one of the characters in its voluminous ensemble. In the earliest days of the creation of the series, the creative team behind *Lost* -- co-creators Damon Lindelof and JJ Abrams, with the assistance of Paul Dini, Christian Taylor, Jennifer Johnson, and myself -- came upon the idea of using flashbacks to develop the operational themes for each character. The flashbacks to the crash of Oceanic 815 first presented in the pilot transformed into full-blown plots extending through the course of the series. The island stories were presented in direct contrast to who the characters were in their former everyday lives: every action in the island present became an attempt to compensate for shortcomings in the past's real world.

The operating theme of *Lost* is simple and applies to every character: Who do you say you are when you can reinvent yourself with impunity? Every member of the *Lost* ensemble was living a lie on the island. These lies dictated their behavior and led them to try -- either successfully or unsuccessfully -- to remake themselves into their most desired version of themselves.

Jack strove to lead in spite of a life of personal failure and the scorn of an unloving father. Kate yearned to prove herself a good person in spite of being a wanted criminal. Michael tried to be an able parent after being absent from his son's entire life. Charlie struggled to be a caretaker to Claire and her unborn child while concealing his drug addiction. John Locke -- mysteriously healed of his paralysis by the island -- was hell-bent on proving himself a man of action and principle after a lifetime of meek submission. Sun pretended to be a dutiful Korean wife, concealing even her fluency in the English from the brutal husband -- whose brutality itself was a smokescreen to conceal a deep yearning for his own broken dreams -- whom she was preparing to escape. The list goes on.

What's important is that every character had the *same* operational theme. The synthesis of personal desire for reinvention in contrast to the reality of each character's previous life propelled one story after another for the course of *Lost*'s first two seasons: 48 hours of television that cemented the show's place in the popular culture.

The operational theme of *Lost* -- obvious as it seems in retrospect -- did not become clear to the creative team until after the pilot had been shot and we were tasked with figuring out *how* exactly the series would work in episode after episode. We were very close to falling prey to the fallacy that makes for the downfall of most of the proposed serialized sci-fi pilots that come down the pike: we were almost -- almost -- seduced by a shiny concept -- the mysteries of the island, from the smoke monster to the presence of ghosts from the past in the present. We almost focused on the mystery instead of the operational theme of the characters.

To this day, I thank God we had the epiphany early.

By dealing with the unknown, beguiling, and generally spectacular (aliens! robots! vampires! alien robot vampires!), sci-fi as a genre has the sneaky ability to fool otherwise extremely capable writers into believing that a nifty concept with a lot of unanswered questions is enough to carry a television series. It isn't.

To have something spectacular take place -- the arrival of aliens, a space/time conflagration that causes everyone to see a few minutes of their future, a plane crash in a mysterious island -- and then spend 22 episodes showing how the characters figure out merely what happened, how, and whether it can be fixed, is not only the biggest failure of the imagination possible in sci-fi drama, it is also an insult to the genre. It assumes that sci-fi is somehow "easier" than a deeply character-driven, kitchen-sink realist narrative (like *Mad Men*) that requires the protagonist to have a rich inner life in order to motivate conflict.

The island on *Lost* served the same purpose as the ad agency on *Mad Men*: it was a space where the protagonist sought to invent a new life in spite of all evidence to the impossibility of that endeavor. The conspiracy in *Orphan Black* is nothing more or less than a perfect physicalization of a young woman's struggle to define her own identity: one which just so happens to cause her to come into conflict and allegiance with numerous clones of herself, all of them living vastly different lives with remarkably different outcomes.

Many big and shiny ideas can tap dance around a lack of an operational theme for a while -- the length of a pilot, maybe even a season of decompressed cable-style narrative. But no amount of spectacle can obscure the truth that a protagonist or ensemble with a stark, robust, and recognizable operational theme is the source of all televisual drama.

Ironically, sci-fi, the genre that most often suffers from underdeveloped characters on TV, probably demands more *character* from its characters than any other genre. Why? Because it is, at the core, a metaphorical exercise. Sci-fi poses a question that extends beyond the easily understandable stakes of the cop, doctor, or lawyer. How are the aliens, robots, mysterious islands, viral outbreaks, and vampires an external manifestation of your main character's self-concept?

If you are writing a genre pilot and your premise can't answer that question -- while placing your protagonist in a place where the pursuit of their most prescient emotional issue is in consistent, discernible, and direct opposition of those aliens, robots, islands, viral outbreaks, and vampires -- then, like any other writer in any other genre, you have to dig deeper. Because the privilege of having a scholar find and explain your lofty thematic concern like "power," "alienation," or (still my personal favorite,) "the shallowness of modern life" doesn't come right away.

Scholars and bloggers don't proclaim the deep meaningful metaphors of your creation if you have not done the hard spade-and-trowel labor of putting an interesting main character on the screen. You must first put your characters in the one, singular (and preferably, for my money, science-fictional!) situation that *most* challenges their true self.

That's your operational theme -- a weekly duel against your character's innermost identity. It is knowing the one thing your protagonist's needs more than anything else in the world and then putting him or her in the scenario most likely to deprive them of it for years to come: a feat of creative invention that will sustain hour after hour of narrative storytelling, season after season -- preferably to the delight of millions of viewers, the acclaim of hundreds of critics, and the munificence of a murder of blue-chip advertisers.

To create a successful show -- to find the next *Lost* -- you must not only have the High Concept, you must find that perfect puzzle-piece of a protagonist -- the one whose innermost need most conflicts with the worst case scenario of your High Concept... and when you find that...

Have your agent call my agent.

MY YEAR WITHOUT STAR WARS

Originally published by io9.com on December 29, 2010.

Thirteen months ago, during a prolonged bout with depression, I was visited -- Ebenezer Scrooge-like -- by a trio of revelations that changed the course of my life.

Back then, my palliative for emotional stress was to drag out my laser disc of *The Empire Strikes Back*. For years, anyone close to me would know I was wrestling the black dog if they could hear John Williams' Wagnerian chords in the background of a phone call. On this night, however, I popped in a DVD of *Revenge of the Sith* -- for no reason other than my ongoing fascination with the densely populated, single-take, opening space battle sequence.

Two minutes and 30 seconds into this -- my 47th -- viewing, I had the same disturbing thought from every viewing since my first (when -- well into my thirties -- I insisted on vacation that my father drive me from the far shores of Maui to see it opening weekend).

It always came at the same moment; when the brilliant space battle choreographed by a hundred CGI artists -- all presumably my age and inspired to creative careers by a shared vision of a weirdly democratic, yet profoundly aristocratic dreamland of glow-sword-wielding superheroes and pistol-packin' everymen -- is replaced by a poorly-composed close-up of Hayden Christensen reciting nonsensical dialogue against a green screen.

I was usually able put the thought aside... but on this night, it spoke with the *basso profundo* of a Dickensian apparition. The deep voice of an authority even bigger than James Earl Jones had been sent on a mission to take a flame thrower to my fandom.

It was the Ghost of Christmas Past. This is what it said to me:

"Schmuck. You saw *The Phantom Menace* six times in the theater, then invested in the letterboxed VHS when Uncle George announced there would be no DVD. You even sprang for the Japanese import laserdisc because you convinced yourself the reason you don't enjoy it is that you missed out on something in the first dozen viewings. Then -- like a dutiful Soviet-era Muscovite -- you bought the DVD when Lucasfilm finally deigned to release it. You watched it some 20 more times because you thought you were in a bad mood -- or looked away at the wrong time -- the first 25 and just didn't 'get it.' Take *Attack of the Clones* and *Revenge of the Sith*. Rinse and repeat.

It is time to face the truth...

The prequels suck, and no amount of repeat viewing is going to change that."

There followed the shrill, sibilant voice of Christmas Present:

"You have seen these six films more times than you have had sex."

OK. That's funny because it's sad, and sad because it's true. Let's move on to the Ghost of Christmas Future:

"You have nothing left to learn here. You must spend a year without *Star Wars*. Only then will you understand."

"A YEAR without *Star Wars*? No scruffy-lookin' nerf-herdin' way! I'm a true believer!"

Yes, a True Believer.

Let me explain. For a decade-and-change, "George Lucas raped my childhood" has been the rallying cry of many a disaffected Gen-X/Y-er whose dreams of a repeat performance of their age-of-10-stand-up-and-cheer-movie-going-experience were dashed by the prequels.

To those who have said it, I have one thing to say, and it comes from the heart:

Fuck you.

George Lucas didn't rape a Goddamn thing. He GAVE me my childhood. He provided the fat, pale, and sensitive boy I once was with a vibrant, imaginative and optimistic idea of what storytelling could be. George Lucas engineered a waking dream that evolved into an overwhelming desire to become a creator on my own right. I am where I am thanks, in great part, to George Lucas. I went to the University of Southern California film school because that's where he went. I make TV, films and comics because he showed me that it is possible. If I should ever meet the guy, I will shake his hand and thank him... then go about my business... without making further eye contact.

Like I said, I'm a True Believer. How could I spend a YEAR without *Star Wars*?

Some would argue the issue of artistic intent or lack thereof. They'd say the prequels were a cash grab. They'd ask "Who does George Lucas think he is to continually revisit and revise his work to sell it back to his fans?" Followed by "and did there really have to be that many Expanded Universe books?"

My answer to them is also simple. Who gives a shit?

Are we really entitled to have "the originals" at our disposal because we shelled out at a proto-multiplex back in 1977 and liked what we saw? The privilege to have a piece of artistic work at our fingertips, exactly the way we remember it, on-demand and in real-time, is so modern an idea that we have absolutely no way to say for certain to what it is that we have the right. No one has had that right at any other time in history. What makes us such special snowflakes?

So shut the door and have a seat, children. Here's a slice of reality pie: it's Uncle George's work. As much as we perceive it a vital part of our archetypal mindscape, he has the right to revise, expurgate, monetize, and three-dimensionalize to his heart's content, and there is nothing we can do about it. It just doesn't belong to us.

And yet -- argued my *Star Wars*-lovin' soul -- you CAN'T have a year without *Star Wars*!

Star Wars is the pop-cultural air we breathe! Especially now that those of us between the ages of 35 and 45 are becoming the writers, directors, producers and show-runners at the forefront of popular culture. The mythical language of *Star Wars* -- aided and abetted by Joseph Campbell -- is the DNA of many a modern creator's understanding of story and character. It is the double helix of current media, repeated endlessly in both jokes and references as well as a generation's understanding of the Gross Anatomy of narrative.

The Ghosts had receded. It was now my intellect versus my soul.

My intellect took the ball and ran with it:

Star Wars is the monomyth of Gens- X and Y: so pervasive that it occupies the mental volume whole genres did in the past. In some future accounting of late twentieth and early twenty-first century popular entertainment the term *Star Wars* could be spoken in the same way we now say "the Western."

Star Wars isn't entertainment: it is a language, and anyone with access to the internet, DVD, VHS, Super-8, or two cans attached by a string can share in the conversation.

As members of an audience, millions of us feel that *Star Wars* speaks to and for us. We made it a touchstone and a way of life. George Lucas may be rich enough to own half of Marin County, but we gave him our minds and money. In our gluttonous lust to replicate the exhilaration of a matinee from 1977, we demanded that his otherwise fun little film metastasize into so pervasive a chunk of the collective unconscious that Carl Jung now sports Mandalorian armor and flies a modified Firespray-31 attack cruiser turned slave ship.

And how in high unholy hell can I cite the make and model of Boba Fett's ship in conversation? The words "Mandalorian," "Firespray-31," or "Ewok" for that matter aren't in these films! Listen to your brain, nerd: you NEED a year without *Star Wars*!

Of course, the part of me that loves *Star Wars* wasn't letting go. These films helped me identify and cement my vocation. How could there be NOTHING left to learn about the craft of moviemaking from the scores of wizards involved in these films? How dare I?

Surely more repeat viewings were necessary... or maybe re-reading some of the ancillary works of the Expanded Universe (like the eBooks set in the aftermath of the Yuuzhan Vong invasion of known space)... or the graphic novels a 150 years ABY... or maybe I needed to use my industry contacts to seek out some of those scripts for the long-rumored *Star Wars* drama series set in the criminal underbelly of Coruscant.

I finally heard myself. I was an addict. Extreme detox

was the only way out.

The conditions coalesced quickly. I would spend a year without consuming any *Star Wars*-branded content (excluding the odd viral video or such impossible-to-miss things as billboards or cosplay at Comic-Con). No ifs, ands, or buts.

It wasn't as hard as I imagined. As someone who has struggled with weight and body image since age eight, deprivation is a welcome masochism. Becoming a manorexic of *Star Wars* is, frankly, a less daunting thought for me than renouncing the bread basket at the top of every meal.

I was, however, pained to decline a good friend's invite to see a new print of *The Empire Strikes Back* projected at LA's revered Arclight Cinema with a special Q&A with Harrison Ford.

Then again, two years earlier, I saw a new print of *The Empire Strikes Back* projected at LA's revered Arclight Cinema with a special Q&A by Irvin Kershner.

Fandom charges you for the same experience a billion times over while fooling you into believing you are getting special and exclusive content... and, shame on us, we shell out again and again.

For 12 months, I made a similar calculus every time the opportunity to consume *Star Wars* came along.

By and large my "year without *Star Wars*" passed without tears, debilitating anxieties or the black shakes of withdrawal... OK, except for the one night when I woke up at 4 A.M. and listened to "Battle of the Heroes" on my iPod, sue me...

...and after 12 months, I didn't hook up the laserdisc player and drown my ongoing sorrows in *The Empire Strikes Back*. *Star Wars* had quietly left the forefront of my mind -- and now exists solely as a memory of the lightning-in-a-bottle event that crystallized my desire to do what I now do.

It wasn't until a good month later that I casually popped in my DVD of *Revenge of the Sith* to show off my sound system to a visiting friend. Then I turned it off and went about my day, without giving it any further thought.

I know what you're thinking: "OK -- you just spent endless words bragging about how you threw your metaphorical Emperor down the symbolic shaft of your personal Death Star, you wanna tell us what you learned so we can go dance with the Ewoks?"

Lesson #1: the longer I stay away from *Star Wars*, the more annoyed I am by its ubiquity.

In my willing estrangement from Luke Skywalker and his merry band of rebels, I came to value their small and very personal adventure in contrast to the massive cultural apparatus it spawned. It now seems absurd that a film as sparsely populated -- one whose triumph of the imagination was to imply massive scope through the judicious use of production design, location and editing while telling a relatively small hero's journey story -- has developed so overwhelming a cultural footprint.

Where before, a character's despair at being sent to the "Spice Mines of Kessel" sparked an electrical storm of imagination ("Spice? Like oregano? How does one MINE oregano? And why are the working conditions so deplorable?"), now every corner of that universe has been strip-quarried for character, incident, and action-figure design. As a seven-year-old, Star Wars was a Tesla coil of wonder.

Thirty-four years later, it's more like Mervyn Peake's *Gormenghast*: a hulking repository of arcana picked over by an ever-expanding army of courtiers who have lost sight of the original principle. The Spice Mines of Kessel now have a gift shop, Starbucks and an Etsy tent where locals sell homemade tees with delightfully witty silkscreens of Wilhuff Tarkin in the style of Shepard Fairey.

And you know why that is? Not because Uncle George is a bad man who loves filthy lucre -- but because we demanded it.

Now comes Lesson #2.

As the creator of a TV series regarded by detractors as a 16-car-pileup of geeky references without human meaning, I can only evoke the ancient Vulcan proverb "Only Nixon could go to China" when I write the following line:

I'm sick and tired of all the inside jokes and references.

There was a long ago and far, far away time -- I think it was the early '90s -- when a character in a film saying "I have a bad feeling about this," or "That's no moon, that's a space station," was an adorable grace note. Today, entire episodes of TV and whole feature films are devoted to *Star Wars* references. Even the most high-minded and hard-edged 10 o'clock procedurals manage to get in a winkety-wink-wink. Worse yet, the franchise's own prequels, sequels, and equals -- all the attendant films, books, TV shows and graphic novels -- are equally full of inside jokes and callbacks to the original. The Hutt isn't just eating its own tail, it's serving it to itself on a silver platter with drawn butter and a finger bowl.

One of the many films I re-watched during my Year Without *Star Wars* was Wim Wenders' *Until the End of the World*. Among that story's many rambling flights of conceptual fancy is a subplot concerning "the disease of images." Having stumbled on a way to record their own dreams on digital tape, the protagonists became obsessed with watching them played back over and over again to the point of addiction, social dissociation, and toxic self-obsession.

The cure for the disease of images is the creation of new narratives -- described by one character as "the healing power of words and stories."

I now wonder if the same isn't true about the entertainment industry's relationship to *Star Wars*. How many modern blockbusters seem like cargo cult versions of that childhood inspiration? How many "tentpole" blockbusters consist of the same images repeated over and over again telling no new tale?

How many times do I have to walk out of a theater thinking: "I just paid to see a laundry list of beats that 'worked' in *Star Wars*" before wondering if our collective doorway to archetypal storytelling hasn't become a Trojan Horse?

In too many cases, the structure has become the content. *Star Wars* may have taught the Hero's Journey to entire generations, but it is our responsibility to use the paradigm and to forge something with its own emotional integrity. Structure should be armor -- the protection that makes it safe to seek out originality in the dangerous tunnels where raw matter is buried -- not a pop-culture sign-post indicating where the emotional content would have gone in the hands of a writer with a broader frame of reference.

All creators imitate, emulate, and steal. All maturing artists engage in a dialogue with what came before... but I can't think of a single instance in history when so many of us are so actively engaged in paying homage to a single work of art. Bluntly: we are all cribbing our best moves from the same two-hour movie and it has to stop. There just isn't enough meat on the carcass.

Lesson #3: My otaku-like obsession with the *Star Wars* universe cheapened the emotional force of the original.

The most important lesson I needed from *Star Wars* I learned when I lifted my index finger to the screen and exclaimed "I want to do that." A gifted visionary -- under the right conditions, with the right collaborators and an openness to their feedback -- can create transcendent art that will change lives. Everything else is candy. Sweet, delightful, and comforting, but no basis for what your people call "a life debt." After 34 years, I was ready to shed the spare tire around the metaphorical midriff of my mental space.

Lesson #4 was the toughest.

A few months ago, I received a package of DVDs of *The Chronicle*, a little-seen, low-budget sci-fi show I wrote for in the early naughties. After watching my episodes in a bout of unbridled Norma Desmond-osity I found myself uncharacteristically happy.

I shook hands with my younger self. I made peace with my flaws -- the derivative plotting, jokes for their own sake, crow-barring in of arch dialogue I knew wouldn't sound natural, and, naturally, an annoyingly huge number of *Star Wars* references. I forgave my past self these indulgences and incompetencies and enjoyed the encounter -- not out of arrogance, but an appreciation of how much fun I had back then and how far I've come.

There's a term that goes with being able to appreciate one's past and not dwell on the flaws as if they represent a judgment on one's current value as a person. I heard it may be "self-esteem."

When the *Star Wars* Trilogy Special Edition was

released in 1997, I was hardly a naysayer. I saw all three on opening night at Mann's Chinese and rationalized the "enhancements" as a "cost of doing business." Sure "Jedi Rocks" was lame, but worth it to have a print of *The Empire Strikes Back* without the see-through snow-speeders. During my year without *Star Wars*, however, I realized how much The Maker's constant tinkering with his own creation truly pushes my buttons. Even if the originals are freely available on demand and in real time, even if I know that they are his to do with as he pleases, one question just keeps nagging: why can't he let it be?

I have no intention to pop-psychoanalyze my idol. I don't know the man and haven't walked a mile in his moccasins. This has nothing to do with him, and everything to do with of my reception of his actions.

As someone who has painfully, over the course of many years and many failures -- and much, much psychotherapy -- managed to cobble together détente with the past, I have a hard time with someone so hellbent on erasing perceived mistakes. While I can't possibly understand the what drives a man who at a young age single-handedly changed the face of popular culture and was catapulted to a level of fame that would boggle the mind of a mere journeyman television writer, I suffer for having so close a relationship with the work of someone so preoccupied with an ever-so-elusive ideal of aesthetic perfection that he stamps out what made it great in the first place.

The only thing that matters in my own life is to move forward: to develop beyond what I have already done, to find new ways to express what meager gifts I have -- and to show my past self a little compassion. Past Javi had problems enough as it was: living in fear of the eventual judgment of a future self is a Moebius loop of mental fuckery that could only lead to insanity.

The creative life with which I want communion as an adult is one lived by the principle described by Raul Julia's character in the obscure 1976 film *The Gumball Rally*. Playing a lecherous Ferrari driver, Julia takes the pilot seat, tears out the rearview mirror, and declares that "The first rule of Italian driving" is "what's behind me is not important."

So while I respect that George Lucas believes that in some bright pixellated future there exists a perfect version of *Star Wars* that transcends the limited capacities of 1970s analog cinema, I just don't want to walk beside him on the journey anymore. I love the past and no longer find a reason to judge it wanting -- not when there's every chance that what lies ahead may actually be, you know, fun.

That it took *Star Wars* to teach me that is -- I suppose -- a further credit to the scope of Uncle George's talent and the breadth of his vision... and someday I will fish out the component cables that connect my Pioneer auto-flipping laserdisc player to my TV, pop in my original *Star Wars* platter and spend a lazy afternoon becoming reacquainted with young Luke Skywalker, Han Solo and Princess Leia...

And there -- in a long ago, far-away galaxy of visible matte lines, continuity errors, bad latex masks, kit-bashed models, and herky-jerky flights through star fields indicated by backlit pinholes in black cloth -- I also hope to meet a chubby seven-year-old Puerto Rican misfit who dreams of leaving his remote island home for a bright center of the galaxy in which filmmakers work in concert to make dreams a reality.

I will tell him to watch these movies as many times as he wants.

I AM A FUCKING PLAGIARIST

"Art is theft."
-- **Pablo Picasso**

Before I had anything to say, I had the desire to say something.

No, let me revise that. I had the desire to be heard.

One of the family legends is that at the age of three I leaped on stage during my brother's elementary school Christmas pageant and launched into an extemporaneous monologue in which I apparently demanded that the audience answer for being in my mother's house. My very own toddlerized version of that Dean Martin bit where he steps up to the mic, starts at the sight of the audience, and asks "How'd you all get in here?"

My God. Even at three I was a plagiarist.

"Plagiarism is basic to all culture"
-- **Pete Seeger**

Plagiarist. The word is a snake. Writers loathe its greasy venom. All our worst nightmares begin with the accusation of plagiarism. Why? Because it impugns the myth that we are "original" and therefore "special" and "different"... but even worse because it lives next-door to the one we most suspect to be truth: "fraud."

To further torture the metaphor, "fraud" is a crack house -- an urban blight easily turned from because it exists at an extreme so far from most people's experience. You can always say: "That's not me, I'm not an addict and a criminal" and as long as your shoes, clothes and teeth are passable, have some benefit of the doubt.

"Plagiarist," however, is the lawyer's mansion with the obsessive-compulsively manicured lawn, mirrored hardwood floors, and massive library. "Plagiarist" is a rich and burnished space of unlimited resources, where a methodical investigator -- a latter-day George Smiley -- has made his fortune exposing everyone else... and it's only a matter of time before he turns his unblinking sight on you.

And the insidiously magnificent thing about the word "plagiarist" -- as opposed to, say, "plagiarizer" -- is the sinister double implication of mastery and serial offense. There's something about that -*ist* at the end. It tops the insult off with the injury of "and these are just the ones we've caught... but we're on to you now."

To this day I suspect, in the darkest corners of my guilty soul, that the cottage industry of quotes from famous writers and intellectuals endorsing some form of theft as the only way to evolve the culture is little else than a great, collective, preemptive strike. I'm reminded of the greatest, and most frequently ignored, truth in the PR business: "Go ugly early."

"Go ugly early" basically means "Own it before they catch you."

For example: had Bill Clinton admitted to his infidelities before the media caught on -- the strategy goes -- the scandal would have been short-circuited by blunt and factual admission. Tawdry speculation dies when perpetrators shine a harsh, specular light on their unpleasant truths and take responsibility.

For the plagiarist, the "early" in "Go ugly early"

means "any time before someone else busts you." Hence, I believe, all the quotes. The more flowery your defense of your own plagiarism before the truth comes out, the better. The more flowery your defense after, the more you come off looking like a fucking douche.

It's all in the timing, you see.

> *"Our souls as well as our bodies are composed of individual elements which were all already present in the ranks of our ancestors. The 'newness' in the individual psyche is an endlessly varied recombination of age-old components."*
> **-- Carl Jung**

Twelve years after the "Dean Martin incident," I was a sophomore in high school. Bringing Great Honor to my people (a line I just stole from Mark Leyner's bio page in his novel *My Cousin, My Gastroenterologist*), I was also co-founder and president of "Lunchbox Theater." Tired of not being cast in our high school drama team productions by a faculty coach who hated the smug sight of me, I worked with another student on the idea of a side project for the school's drama team.

(Her name was Stacie Ressler, and to this day she'd probably tell you I never gave her enough credit for our joint venture.)

The idea? We would write and perform short plays during the lunch recess, thus giving students the ability to, well... be heard.

Taking the sum of our ideas home, I quickly typed a proposal on my mother's Royal typewriter, waved it in front of the drama coach's face and -- based on her most

cursory and dismissive wave-off of tentative approval
-- scheduled a meeting with the school principal to get
permission to launch the project.

The meeting with the principal went like gangbusters.
By the time our drama coach -- a gloriously overworked
sexagenarian with a vindictive streak mitigated by her
rapidly eroding memory -- realized what was going on,
our first play, written by yours truly, was in production
and the posters announcing the premiere were up in the
school hallways.

Score one for the rebels.

This first play was called "Flicks" -- and fitting for
someone too young to have anything to say -- it was about
a movie mogul whose work was constantly interrupted
by assorted caricatures of "industry types" inasmuch as I
understood them. It was essentially a 10 minute vignette of
even shorter vignettes taken from my impression of how
Hollywood "worked" based on my obsessive viewing of
the then-nascent *Entertainment Tonight*.

To everyone's surprise but mine, "Flicks" attracted
something of an audience. The smattering of applause
we received was ultimate confirmation that my end run
around our tyrannical drama coach had been a righteous
move. It was also my first taste of that most addicting of
sensations -- the dragon everyone who puts pen to paper is
chasing even if they want you to believe otherwise.

I had been heard.

I was also immediately overtaken by a sense of abject
dread. Later in life, as a working television writer, I would
come to understand that tensing of the chest as the natural
condition of all life on Earth. This was our first show. We
had committed to doing one of these plays every other
week.

What were we going to do for an encore?

"Nothing is original. Steal from anywhere
that resonates with inspiration or fuels
your imagination. Devour old films, new
films, music, books, paintings, photographs,
poems, dreams, random conversations,
architecture, bridges, street signs, trees,
clouds, bodies of water, light and shadows.
Select only things to steal from that
speak directly to your soul. If you do this,
your work (and theft) will be authentic.
Authenticity is invaluable; originality is
nonexistent."
   -- Jim Jarmusch

At the end of my junior year, I stepped down from the Lunchbox troupe's leadership to make a bid for the student presidency of the greater drama team: a move so dreaded by our coach that her final act before announcing her retirement was to follow up my campaign speech with a stern announcement that the other students "not vote for friendship, but for the best person for the job."

To this day, I appreciate her vast overestimation of my popularity. The way she tipped her hand was among the greatest validations I ever received from an adult.

It's one thing to be complimented for your academic performance, or even your moxie, but to have inspired fear? In a mighty grown-up no less? By putting up a couple of shitty amateur sketches? Now THAT was the kind of trouble to which all artists aspire. I was her own personal Tracy Flick.

Except I lost the election.

So I settled into an emeritus role at Lunchbox Theater, producing and directing as many short plays as I could write. I could no longer pretend to be an outcast malcontent. I had become a generally popular member of the student body, the co-creator of a popular theater program, and pulling double duty as features editor of the school paper.

Even better, our new drama coach turned out to be an extraordinarily supportive mentor with a remarkable way of simultaneously encouraging me, giving me enough rope to hang myself, and calling me out on my general stupidity and arrogance.

I even went on a few dates and acquired written proof that at least one girl at the school found me "very handsome."

By the time Huron High School released me, Lunchbox Theater had become an institution that would go on for almost a decade and a half after my graduation, and the yearly "Lunchbox Theater Festival" -- which I had inaugurated after our second year -- had become something of a highlight of the school year.

Moreover, other teachers started to pay attention to our little island of misfit toys... one of them was impressed enough by my leadership and the sheer volume of my output to nominate me for a scholarship from the National Council of Teachers of English. Another one of my teachers wrote a college letter of recommendation I aspire to live up to pretty much every day.

The Xeroxed 8.5-by-11 posters of my accomplishments hung proudly on my childhood bedroom wall alongside posters for Lucas and Spielberg films. The titles of my plays were as silly as adolescence: "Flicks," "Suburban Life," "Table Talk," "The Incredible Frampster," "King

Rex," "Son of Rex," "The Date," "The Incredible
Adventures of the Intrepid Teddy Potsdorf," "Son of the
Incredible Adventures of the Intrepid Teddy Potsdorf."

Out of that collection, point your attention to title
number two: "Table Talk."

That's my original sin. The act of plagiarism that
defines my self-concept to this day. It is the smoking gun
whose discovery I have spent three decades fearing.

> *"I don't think that you saw me do those*
> *jokes and said, 'I'm going to tell those jokes,*
> *too.' I don't think there's a world where*
> *you're that stupid. Or that bad a guy... I do*
> *think, though, that you're like... a rocket...*
> *and your engines are sucking stuff up. Stuff*
> *is getting sucked up in your engines, like*
> *birds and bugs and some of my jokes. I think*
> *you saw me do them. I know you saw me*
> *do them, and I think they just went in your*
> *brain, and I don't think you meant to do*
> *it, but I don't think you stopped yourself*
> *either."*
>
> **-- "Louie" to "Dane Cook" fictionally addressing**
> **real-world accusations of plagiarism of Louis**
> **CK's material by Cook. From the episode "Oh**
> **Louie/Tickets" of** *Louie*

These are the facts:

On May 15 of 1982, the third-to-last sketch of *Saturday
Night Live* was a two-hander entitled "Table Talk."

The premise: cast member Tony Rosato played a
rough-around-the-edges vulgarian food critic using a
first-person, break-the-fourth-wall monologue to teach the

audience how to defraud good restaurants of their wine. A less-than-competent waiter served as his foil. The sketch ended with Rosato telling the audience to tune in next week when he would teach them how to "stuff an entire salad bar into a doggie bag."

Sometime in 1986, I wrote a short play about a stuck-up, manners-obsessed restaurant critic using a first-person, break-the-fourth-wall monologue to teach the audience the make-up of a perfect meal and the way a proper restaurant ought to go about serving it. The critic's monologue was continually interrupted by such digressions as a noisy family with children, a tacky lounge singer on a date with a cheesy divorcee, and a Cuban hijacker with Multiple Personality Disorder bent on redirecting the restaurant to Havana. An incompetent waiter and grotesquely stereotypical French *Maitre D'* -- who was more than a little derivative of John Cleese in *Monty Python's The Meaning of Life* -- served as his foils.

"Table Talk" was performed three times by Lunchbox Theater: it premiered during a lunchtime recess in the fall semester and was subsequently revived as a curtain-raiser for the drama team's spring production, and for the year-end festival. During my freshman year at Carnegie Mellon University, I convinced the extracurricular drama club to perform the play in one of the school's restaurants.

"Table Talk" had its swan song in 1992 when the Flaming Gorilla Company -- a troupe I formed with my friends to perform new work during the summers between college semesters -- decided to go out with a bang by making our last ever production a charity event/nostalgia fest for our high school theater company: "The Original Lunchbox Theater Festival."

By the time this final production came around, "Table

Talk" had metastasized to include the scene-stealing
addition of an explosively flatulent restaurant patron.

> *"Immature poets imitate; mature poets*
> *steal; bad poets deface what they take, and*
> *good poets make it into something better, or*
> *at least something different. The good poet*
> *welds his theft into a whole of feeling which*
> *is unique, utterly different from that from*
> *which it was torn; the bad poet throws it*
> *into something which has no cohesion."*
> **-- TS Eliot**

I have a great memory -- maybe not photographic, but
definitely classical realist. I can't tell you with a straight
face that I didn't remember I hadn't seen the *SNL* sketch
when I sat down to write my "Table Talk" on that Royal
typewriter at two in the morning on a dateless Friday
night. That would be a lie.

Yes. I knew it. It's why I went out of my way to write
something radically different. I even considered changing
the title to "Dinner Mints" because I realized in the
forefront of my mind that, while I found the alliterative
title positively beguiling, it would -- quite rightfully -- raise
the dreaded specter of plagiarism.

To this day, I wish I had. I also wonder if I would be a
different person for it.

The one thing I can't figure out no matter how hard I
rack my brain is whether I was a dumb kid who just sort
of figured "who the hell has ever heard of this *Saturday
Night Live* show anyway," or whether I believed that I had
changed so much of the structure and content of what I
had seen that I convinced myself the title wasn't going to

matter...

Or whether I perversely reasoned that I had earned the right to keep the title because I had made so many "improvements" on the concept.

There are dark places in the mind that stubbornly resist the effort to excavate the irritating artifact whose removal will provide relief. Or maybe it's just that there is no artifact and no relief is possible.

Maybe I just wanted to be heard.

I do know this: after the play went up for the first time, a girl on whom I harbored a massive crush asked me if I had ever seen a similarly-themed sketch on *Saturday Night Live* a few years before. I denied all knowledge.

Before that, when my friends would call me out on quoting Monty Python or *SCTV* too liberally -- which, by the way, was <u>invariably</u> -- or whether I had invented my superhero "Galactic Cow" in the sixth grade not just out of a bovine obsession born of multiple childhood trips to my great uncle Vicente's dairy farm, but also a misguided admiration of the Ted Knight sitcom *Too Close for Comfort*, I would generally sheepishly cop to it and go on my way without much moral injury.

Frankly, I wish I had admitted to it and either retitled or withdrawn the play altogether, because I now believe it was at that moment -- and not when I conceived of the possibility of making a thing taking themes from a sketch I had seen on a show one time -- that I truly shamed myself.

I was a plagiarist already -- but that's the moment I became a fucking plagiarist.

> *"All writing is in fact cut-ups. A collage of*
> *words read heard overheard. What else?"*
> **-- William S. Burroughs**

In the mid aughts, then-Harvard sophomore Kaavya Viswanathan received what was widely reported as a half-million dollar-plus contract for a novel she wrote in high school -- *How Opal Mehta Got Kissed, Got Wild, and Got a Life* -- and a projected sequel. The real-life story was sensational headline-bait: a high-achieving young woman of color writing an exceptional book about her coming-of-age experiences and getting richly rewarded for her hard work.

High-profile agents at William Morris and a movie deal followed...

Until the entire shitbox came crashing down when it was revealed that many passages of her book bore a striking resemblance to the work of well-established and respected YA novelist Megan McCafferty.

Several excruciating months of accusations, denials, and outright class warfare followed. The color of her skin aside, Viswanathan's "superhero origin story" was chock full of signifiers of wealth and privilege: her parents, both physicians, had spent thousands to hire an "admissions coach" to help her get into Harvard, and it was this person who first recognized her literary genius. And let's face it, there's a dedicated wing at the Cooperstown of Being Insufferable for that special breed of Harvard grad that can't resist but name-check their alma mater within the first five minutes of any conversation. Cowed resignation followed, Viswanathan was duly, and -- my waggish tone notwithstanding -- rightfully, shamed.

Her book was pulled from the shelves and pulped.

By the time the dust settled and all the online and mainstream media outlets had their way with the carcass, Viswanathan had been proven beyond the shadow of a doubt to have not only lifted passages from McCafferty's

novels *Sloppy Firsts* and *Second Helpings*, but also from
Meg Cabot's *The Princess Diaries*, Tanuja Desai Hidier's
Born Confused, Sophie Kinsella's *Can You Keep a Secret?*,
and even Salman Rushdie's *Haroun and the Sea of Stories*.
The Collective Detective -- that legion of crime-busting
journalists professional and amateur, armed with Google,
PDFs, searchable eBook editions of the western canon
-- had judged her not just a plagiarist, but a fucking
plagiarist.

In her own defense, Viswanathan claimed that, yes,
she had read those books, but that as she wrote her novel,
she truly believed that she was writing her own voice and
experience. Further along the line, she also explained that
-- because she does in fact have a photographic memory
-- it was quite possible that, in the rush of creation,
her prodigious mental capacity did too good a job of
transposing her experience of reading into those places
where the words corresponded to her experience of life.

When I was in the ninth grade, a substitute music
teacher suggested to our choir that the way to "get good"
at anything creative was to mimic the work of the masters.
He even gave the example of how, when he was our age
and learning his craft, he played his clarinet along to
Benny Goodman records -- matching Goodman note-for-
note -- until he achieved proficiency.

Now, I'd love to sell you on the notion that my
"misunderstanding" of this kind man's generous advice
is what led to my crimes, but that would be unfair to him,
and would let me off the hook way too easily. No, I need
his words to make another point entirely that does not
exonerate me in any way, but rather to ask a question...

How does a zygotic writer "play along to Benny
Goodman?"

Around the same time as the Viswanathan scandal, another writer -- Cassandra Clare -- emerged from a shit storm of often scathing online criticism to publish her first novel *The Mortal Instruments: City of Bones*. Clare's previous incarnation had been as a popular writer of *Harry Potter* fan fiction. Like much other fanfic, her work was chock full of *homage* in the form of lines of dialogue and plot points referencing other fantasy properties.

In Clare's case, the Collective Detective appears convinced that she lifted the form and structure of an entire chapter from another fantasy novel for her own uses as well. She also claims this as *homage*. To the many who vociferously continue to make the detracting case online, Clare's fanfic committed acts of straight-up plagiarism. To her, and her defenders, it simply did what is an essential component of fanfic: to conflate, aggregate, and flatter, its influences through quotation.

Clare had the last laugh on her online critics. Her book series -- which is unrelated to her *Harry Potter* fan fiction other than in being a fantasy portrayal of young people grappling with their entrance into a "hero's journey" paradigm of magic and questing -- has become a publishing phenomenon. Multiple sequels, prequels and equals -- as well as a movie -- followed. A TV series is currently in the works.

Viswanathan went on to law school, where she excelled academically, landed an enviable summer associate position, and presumably continues to flourish. A tragic footnote to her journey is that when her parents perished in an airplane crash in 2011, the story gained some news-cycle traction because of her notoriety.

Do a Google search and imagine yourself in the shoes of someone whose mother and father's sudden and horrible passing at a young age (both were early 50s) was widely reported as the death of the parents of Harvard plagiarist Kaavya Viswanathan.

> *"People are always talking about originality, but what do they mean? As soon as we are born, the world begins to work upon us, and this goes on to the end. What can we call our own except energy, strength, and will? If I could give an account of all that I owe to great predecessors and contemporaries, there would be but a small balance in my favor."*
> **-- Goethe**

I followed the Viswanathan plagiarism scandal with great interest, and great dread.

As the Collective Detective pulled apart Viswanathan's novel -- finding all of her legitimate lifts from other authors -- I couldn't help but ask myself a question. What young person's creative work -- even one without such flagrant steals -- could possibly hide its influences against that level of fine-toothed scrutiny?

Between high school and college, I wrote or co-wrote some 26 pieces for the stage including one-acts, a full-length play, and the book for a musical, I wrote a weekly column for my college paper, and occasionally contributed movie reviews and an additional editorial column. I even sent back dispatches from a semester in London. I also performed two one-man monologue shows. How is that level of output not going to, in some way, reflect every idea that came under the transom?

Hell, my entire adolescent psyche was an act of

intellectual plagiarism made in rehearsal for something that would eventually become an adult life -- and I dare you, dear reader, to claim that anything you did in your formative years was anything other.

If you read my journals you will find a boy who was certain that he would spend a lifetime upholding the undeniable and enduring value of post-structuralism by way of Eco and Baudrillard... followed by the undeniable and enduring value of Sartrean Existentialism... and then Camusean Existentialism, and then Brechtian Marxism vis-a-vis the theater audience as a metaphor for humanity at large, and then Liberation Theology, and then Ayn Randian Objectivism, and -- by the end of my senior year of college -- morose and resigned Orwellian truth-telling socialism.

I was playing along with Benny Goodman, and the varied institutions responsible for my growth and development threw Benny Goodmans at me as fast as I could listen to their LPs.

Unlike Viswanathan, I had the good fortune of not having anything I wrote mistaken for mature professional work and bought for a fortune. I had the lucky break of not being covered as a phenom by the world press. I had the privilege of not being the voice of my race, class, or generation in anyway whatsoever. What I was given was space to experiment, and -- most importantly -- fail.

Which I did. Often.

I was also lucky for the tutelage of a legion of patient teachers and peers who sometimes by honest criticism and guidance, and others by open derision, forced me to find my own voice as opposed to borrowing those of others. Or at least borrowing without citing.

That's right. Somewhere in that unconscionably protracted period of gestation, even this slow learner caught on to that truth to which the entire world expects all true writers to be born -- because it's clearly a one-strike-and-you're-out offense.

"Thou shalt not be a fucking plagiarist."

It was for the best that it took so long for me to learn this lesson, and even longer to gain some proficiency and become a professional in my field. As any legitimate prodigy will tell you -- accused beneficiary of "nepotism" Lena Dunham comes to mind -- being anointed "child genius" and given a showy and much-publicized financial boon for preternaturally brilliant work is the world's biggest "kick me" sign. Few are hated more than the young, gifted, and perceived as unfairly munificent.

And woe betide the ones lacking the cunning to cover their sins adequately, because these days, the judges, juries and executioners all have Google.

As for Cassandra Clare, a key difference between her and Viswanathan is clear. If Clare did, in fact commit acts beyond mere *homage*, they all took place in the grey-market world of fanfic, which -- Amazon's recent efforts to license intellectual properties in order to give fanfic writers the ability to sell their efforts notwithstanding -- is not for profit, not covered by mainstream media, and has only recently led a very selected few to mass-market glory (as evidenced by EL James, who pioneered her block-busting *Fifty Shades of Grey* series as *Twilight* fanfic, and Clare herself).

The difference between plagiarism and fucking plagiarism, it seems, has as much to do with context, intent, venue, and -- some would say most importantly -- the material gains, as it does the act itself.

Though Clare suffered a great deal of madness, rage, and abuse from a large segment of the *Harry Potter* online fan community, she wasn't exposed to the world at large by journalists, nor was she publicly stripped of her contracts, and labeled a plagiarist by the *New York Times* and others to the point where the indictment would go so far as become the lede in the story of her parents' death. Clare did, apparently, change the spelling of her last name from "Claire" and deleted her fanfic from the web, presumably in order to avoid lingering associations between her "profic" career and the controversies of her previous incarnation.

Clare was smart, or lucky -- or both, or neither -- to do all her throat-clearing, rehearsals for prolificity, and playing along with Benny Goodman, in a world where the watchers are limited to fandom, the financial stakes don't get you labeled the Mozart of the YA world and put a target on your back, and -- at the end of the day -- you are still playing in someone else's sandbox and are not liable unless you turn a profit without permission. It wasn't until she had earned her thick hide -- and, presumably, the ability to mask her influences appropriately -- that Clare moved into the mainstream world of Urban Fantasy.

Of course these are all excuses. Nothing exonerates me for "Table Talk."

I am still a fucking plagiarist.

> *"If you steal from one author, it's plagiarism; if you steal from many, it's research."*
> **-- Wilson Mizner**

Plagiarism may be the only crime in which the cover-up ultimately generates far more profit for the perpetrator than the stolen object.

One of the more interesting aspects of getting my start as a television writer in the pre-Second Golden Era TV of the 1990s was getting to work with a number of people who had cut their teeth back when television was REALLY disreputable: the 1970s and '80s.

Aside from getting the general impression that TV in the '80s was essentially *Mad Men* with cocaine, I found many of my superiors to have a very interesting attitude toward... well, if not plagiarism, at least appropriation.

Among the older generation of executive and co-executive producers, the guys who had worked for Stephen J. Cannell, Glen Larson, and their ilk, the running joke was "television is the <u>original</u> derivative medium."

Among the younger writer/producers occupying the mid-level positions, there was a general disdain for the old guard. Many of them saw themselves as renegades eager to wrest TV from thieving forebears (and many of them did, in fact, help bring about the current Golden Age) and a great deal of their contempt found voice in accusations of plagiarism and fraud.

The most salient accusation was always thrown at "this guy who worked at Cannell."

To this day, no one has conclusively told me who "this guy" was, even though I have heard the story told several times. I sometimes wonder if "this guy who worked at Cannell" was the TV equivalent of "this girl from Canada I met at summer camp."

Anyway, "this guy" was legendary for setting up his 22 episode seasons of television by writing on a white board a list of all the classic films he wanted to rip off that year and handing out the titles as assignments to his staff.

Of course, the guys who told the story about "this guy who worked at Cannell" always portrayed themselves as shocked and horrified by the blatant plagiarism. At the same time, they (just like I have more than once in my own career) gladly took the paycheck to write "the *Die Hard* episode" or "the *Rashomon* episode," and, of course, the hardy perennial, "*The Most Dangerous Game* episode."

One thing was always clear -- even if on occasion we in the rank-and-file are forced to do the bidding of a hack showrunner who has no scruples about being a fucking plagiarist -- those of us who tell the story of "this guy" are never the hacks or the thieves. That's the point of the tale. It's a totemic object of immunity, like on *Survivor.* The dishy tale of "this guy" is a shibboleth that alights to others that we too are in the fraternity of Those Who Know Better.

That's why it's always someone else. That's why it's "this guy who worked at Cannell." We're not the thieves. We are the ones who are self-aware and self-referential. We're the ones who excoriate the thieves and occasionally bear with gritted teeth the stark and unpleasant necessities of our trade. We are the ones who say clever things in the writers room like "yes, you've seen it before, but not with these actors" and "that idea is so brilliant I have NO choice but to steal it and claim it for my own" while we bide our time until we can call the shots and chisel True Original Stories from the living rock of our beloved medium.

Inside every writer lives the fantasy that our worst and most derivative work is the result of someone else's influence.

> *"It's not where you take things from—it's*
> *where you take them to."*
> **-- Jean-Luc Godard**

I will always remember my first year in TV as the one in

which not one, but three major network television shows ripped off *John Carpenter's The Thing*.

The venerable and currently, though erroneously, thought-to-be-above-such-shenanigans *The X-Files* even went as far as to stage their episodic riff on Carpenter's paranoid tale of serial possession by an alien parasite found in the ice near a desolate arctic ice station in... well... an arctic ice station.

They even titled the episode "Ice."

Coming in second was *seaQuest DSV* and... well... that program actually ripped off *John Carpenter's The Thing* <u>twice</u> in the same season. Apparently, the series' warring showrunners each had the same brainstorm individually, and then refused to budge on who would withdraw the script written without the other's knowledge. In one, the cause of the possession of successive crew members was a helmet from the lost continent of Atlantis, in the other, an ancient chest found in an undersea mining colony.

Coming in third was *Earth 2*, which substituted an alien parasite found in the ice for... well, an alien parasite found in the ice.

The ugly truth of the matter is this: as respectable as television may have become in the last 20 years, you still have to produce a crap-ton of hours of entertainment. When the beast must be fed at regular intervals on pain of death, the real test of originality is how far you can stretch the trope until it the trope no longer recognizable as the trope -- preferably while finding some sort of resonant human context to which a broadcast audience of millions of all races, creeds, and colors can relate.

When a show becomes popular and produces 22 hours a year -- for many years -- those who love the show ultimately remember the characters, the great moments they shared, and the few truly stand-out stories in the overall narrative miasma. Few of the fans -- even at their most obsessive-compulsive -- actually remember that the individual story of the episode in which their beloved weekly visitors first kissed, or had some other such watershed moment was probably something as hackneyed the "*The Most Dangerous Game* episode."

The amusing truth of the matter is this: often -- especially in a mature career in a medium with six decades of mass visibility -- you will hear a pitch that is derivative of something that was, itself, derivative of something else that the pitcher is not aware of. More than once I have heard a younger writer say, "do you remember that old episode of *Star Trek: The Next Generation* where Riker passes out in the teaser and wakes up and it's 15 years later and he can't remember anything... and he cleverly realizes that his amnesia is really a Romulan ruse to get him to give up sensitive information?" only to be shocked when told, "yeah, it was a take-off from an even older James Garner movie where he's an Allied spy who passes out before the D-Day invasion, wakes up in England 15 years later and can't remember anything, and cleverly realizes that his amnesia is a German ruse to extract from him the location of the invasion."

And yet there's "Table Talk."

> **"We live among ideas much more than we live in nature."**
> **-- Saul Bellow**

As I walked off the Emmy stage into the dark backstage of the Shrine auditorium with the cast of *Lost* and my fellow writer/producers after earning the award for Best Drama,

I entertained the thought of how quickly and easily all of this could all be taken away from me if anyone found out -- and decided to make a Viswanathanian stink about -- "Table Talk."

It wasn't anomalous for me to entertain that thought at the time. I have dined with that unwelcome guest on the average of three to six times a day, every day, for the past thirty years (alongside other, better known, hits from the depressives' jukebox, including the classics "I hate myself and I want to die" and "oh God, oh God, why was I born such a revolting troll?").

Tick-tock-tick-tock-Table-Talk. Tick-tock-tick-tock-Table-Talk.

"Table Talk" was produced at my university. Even if it was extracurricularly -- for no school grade or profit -- the production was funded by a student activities fee levied to every one of the school's attendees... how do I know the administration won't take back my degree after reading this?

How do I know that the National Council of Teachers of English couldn't retroactively rescind the scholarship that sent me there?

How do I know that when the sixth episode of the second season of *Helix* -- the show on which I have toiled as a co-executive producer for the past two years -- hits the air, someone isn't going to think that my use of the line "this is a cleansing moment of clarity," my little *homage* to Paddy Chayefsky's *Network,* is now beyond the pale in the context of these confessions?

How do I know that the very act of putting these thoughts to keyboard won't result in some sort of archaeological examination of my life's work leading to the final determination that -- as a fucking plagiarist -- I am essentially unfit to continue doing the only thing I have ever wanted to do?

How do I know that someone isn't going to figure that the time has come to gut this son of a bitch once and for all?

> *"There's no negotiating with plagiarists,*
> *Dubbie -- you take credit for a man's ideas,*
> *you rob his spirit!"*
> **-- "The Middleman," from the episode "The Boy-Band Superfan Interrogation" of the television series *The Middleman*, written by Jordan Rosenberg, created by Javier Grillo-Marxuach**

In 2006 marvel Comics asked me to create a new hero. All they wanted was to name the character "Wraith," as they owned the name. I came up the idea of a space zombie -- a dead man whose body was reanimated by an alien entity that remains symbiotically bonded to his skin and consumes the souls of others: a power which the grimly revenge-obsessed Wraith occasionally used to vanquish his foes.

Wraith was *The Man with No Name* in space. At first I loved him in all of his goth glory -- I was certain I had created Wolverine by way of The Dark Knight for the Hot Topic set. When I talked to my editor about the character during the heady early days of the project, we were so excited that we even schemed to see Wraith become one of the "Guardians of the Galaxy" (a comic series that was about to be relaunched in the publishing event of which Wraith was part) in much the same way that Spider-Man had once joined the Fantastic Four.

That was until I told a high school friend about

Wraith's oil-slick black body-suit and poncho-like cloak, his pale skin, white hair, and the polymorphous weapon (sometimes it was a sword, sometimes it was a raygun) he wielded with all his might... and he quickly convinced me that I had ripped off Michael Moorcock's Elric.

OK - to be fair, he didn't "convince" me. He only dropped the suggestion in my mind. My guilty conscience did all the heavy lifting in short order.

Nevertheless, my immediate response was to exasperatedly shriek "I've never read Elric!"

And it was legit. I never had. Seriously -- I have a classical-realist memory and I'd definitely remember reading a whole series of novels about the ultra-violent adventures of a soul-sucking albino goth. And, frankly, if I were to rip off Elric, I would have done more to cover my goddamn tracks than putting the motherfucker in space and changing the color of his eyes from red to black.

But all I could think about was "Table Talk." All I could think about was wanting to make my mark once and for all without being a fucking plagiarist.

On the verge of a full-blown nervous breakdown, I spent a sleepless night doing all the internet research I could on Moorcock's Melnibonéan fantasy stories, trying to figure out how I might have known them -- and combing my own library for clues as to how I might have come up with so an idea so derivative of someone else's work. I became convinced that this was not "Table Talk" all over again, but something far more insidious: a criminal impulse that had, having been tamped down over time, now taken up residence in my unconscious mind.

By the time I called my editor the following morning -- pure confession in my now ragged and sleep-deprived voice, convinced that this was the moment of my final unveiling -- and told him the entire project had to be scrapped, I had also convinced myself that I had ripped off everyone else from Bram Stoker to Anne Rice to Dan Simmons.

Of course, the first my editor asked was "Have you even read Elric?" I replied "Absolutely not!" and that was kind of that. Actually, that wasn't kind of that -- I spent the next 15 minutes trying to convince this poor man that I am a fucking plagiarist... but he just wasn't having it.

Duly talked off the ledge, I hanged up the phone and quickly realized that my world-class meltdown had probably just destroyed both the character's long-term chances and my future in comics. Well, the freakout, but also the truth that I had managed to create an utterly derivative character all by myself.

To this day, when the phone rings from Marvel Comics -- usually in the form of a young and newly installed editor who likes my work from a few years back and thinks it'd be nifty to collaborate -- I open the conversation by asking "Are you sure you want to work with me? You do know I'm crazy, right?"

It's self-fulfillingly self-destructive, I know. But everyone deserves fair warning.

"I'm not gonna sit here and plead not guilty... If you watch comedy eight hours a day, something will register, and it'll come out. And if it happened, I said, 'I apologize. I'll pay you for this.' But I wasn't going out of my way to go fucking grave robbing. 'Cause if you're on top, they're gonna look for your ass... and there's lots of people who took entire mannerisms from

> ***me. It's not something I can get mad about. It's flattery. It's great. When it happens the other way around, you're just supposed to smile."***
>
> **-- Robin Williams, *Rolling Stone* magazine, February 21st, 1991**

It makes perfect sense that my childhood idol was dogged by allegations of plagiarism for much of his professional life.

But you know what I truly loved about Robin Williams? The thing he did that freed my mind and inspired me to be something other than who I was? It was how his turbo-charged brain combined and recombined disparate elements into a cohesive absurdist whole.

The Byzantinely circular, free-associative part of Robin Williams' early, cocaine-fueled work (even though at the time I wouldn't have known cocaine from lemon/lime Tang) was to me what punk rock, a skateboard, and hand-painted Doc Martens were to my way-cooler contemporaries.

Williams' pioneering collage-and-remix bits -- like "Elmer Fudd sings Bruce Springsteen," the "Soviet Suppresions" that kicked off his album *Reality, What a Concept*, his Shakespeare pastiche ("the moon, like a testicle, hangs low in the sky!") the digressive riff where he goes to the prom on acid ("No, Mr. Smith, I'll have Becky back in this dimension real soon! Wings! We've got to get those snakes coming out of your eyes fixed!"), or even how he once greeted a swell of applause from the audience by shouting "GIVE US BARABBAS!" -- hit me with the force of shattering cosmic revelation. All his flights of illogical, yet comedically sensical, and emotionally real, insanity made me feel like I was watching a kindred soul broadcasting Truth from a far more advanced place on the spectrum of consciousness.

Robin Williams' comedy explained the world with the same labyrinthine framework with which I understood popular culture: speed, juxtaposition, and incongruity.

He spoke the way I processed the then-nascent 100-channel universe -- where the still-standing UHF channels routinely programmed *Hazel* in close proximity to *Ultraman,* in close proximity to scrambled, pre-internet soft-core, and a new thing called MTV featured five-minute programs of constantly changing genre 24 hours a day.

In every creator's life there is one icon in the culture who seems to reach out from the television screen, or the stage or page, or the hi-fi speaker and says, "I make a living using the skills you hope to someday develop -- it's OK for you to move ahead, it can be done." Even though it was George Lucas and *Star Wars* that made me want to tell stories for a living, it was Robin Williams -- even though he was a comic and I desired to be something very different -- who showed me how I wanted to tell those stories.

Before you think all the hand-wringing confession that has gone before this was merely a Trojan Horse into yet another think-piece about our post-modern condition of sampling, ripping, appropriating, and recontextualizing, let me make one thing absolutely clear. Robin Williams stole jokes: it wasn't cool, he eventually copped to it, and I consider that example with the same weight as I do what I learned from his rapid-fire comedic stylings.

The reason I bring up Robin Williams is not just to expiate the piece of my psyche on the table, but to suggest that there is another, gentler part of my consciousness that, on occasion, whispers -- in a pacifying Jeff Bridges-like drawl -- something along the lines of "Duuude... go a little easy on yourself, lest you forget, your childhood idol committed suicide... and that Marvel thing's kinda nuts!"

Why shouldn't I be a little more forgiving of the venal sins of my teenaged self?

Seriously, I live in a media universe in which a man who is arguably the most influential filmmaker of the past thirty years emerged from widespread accusations that his first film *Reservoir Dogs* was lifted lock-stock-and-barrel from Ringo Lam's Hong Kong New Wave film *City on Fire...*

A director whose last two films, *Inglourious Basterds* and *Django Unchained,* literally include in their very names the titles of the pulp war film and spaghetti western that served as partial inspirations (*The Inglorious Bastards* and *Django...* and interestingly, the latter was subject to countless rip-offs due to its own success, all bearing the "Django" name in the title)...

Indeed, for the vast majority of my adult life, Quentin Tarantino -- whose mastery of collage is, to be fair, matched only by his peerless ability with dialogue and scene structure -- has been one of, if not THE, standard-bearer for art and innovation in screenwriting. That alone says more than a million online think-pieces about our culture of appropriation.

So why can't I stop hating myself and forgive myself for being a fucking plagiarist?

There are dark places in the mind that stubbornly resist the effort to excavate the irritating artifact whose removal will provide relief. Or maybe it's just that there is no artifact and no relief is possible.

Or maybe I just want to be heard.

Or maybe it's something even worse. Something that is equal parts mercenary and pathetic.

> *"Don't quote other movies. Don't tell a story someone else could tell better."*
> **-- Wim Wenders**

I'm at a friend's birthday party.

A mutual acquaintance -- a fledgling writer who has yet to land her first gig on a television series -- tells me about the various jobs she has taken to make ends meet until her ship comes in. One of the more recent ones was at least fun because it required her to watch TV for a paycheck.

That sounds cool. I ask her to tell me more. She explains that she spent several months watching and transcribing broadcast materials, and writing summaries, for an app commemorating *Saturday Night Live*'s fortieth anniversary.

The app's main selling point? On-demand access to every sketch ever performed by the Not-Ready-For-Primetime-Players and their assorted descendants.

"Every sketch?"

I emit the closest I will ever come to that horrible cliché, the audible gulp.

She smiles, trying to read me. To her, this conversation is about little else than the scope of her work in what was a transiently pleasurable temporary occupation. My mood turns a deeper shade with each passing word as I try to maintain my outward composure. I choke back the black bile rapidly gathering in my throat.

I return home from the party, head for my computer, and type the words "I am a fucking plagiarist."

Time to go ugly early.

"As we manipulate everyday words, we
forget that they are fragments of ancient
and eternal stories, that we are building our
houses with broken pieces of sculptures and
ruined statues of gods."
   -- Bruno Schulz

I'd like to share something with you. Something I learned exactly 48 hours ago when I began researching this piece.

On January 24th, 1976 -- four years before I emigrated to the United States from Puerto Rico, years before the widespread availability of cable television would have allowed me to watch American network TV in my homeland, long before I'd hear the words *"Saturday Night Live,"* or "Robin Williams," and a full eighteen months before the world premiere of *Star Wars,* much less its run in Spanish-language theaters -- the sixth sketch of the eleventh episode of the first season of *Saturday Night Live* featured guest hosts Dudley Moore and Peter Cooke performing one of their celebrated comedy routines from the sixties.

The premise? A food critic attempts to interview the incompetent proprietor of a truly horrible restaurant with hilarious consequences.

The sketch was titled "Table Talk."

"Don't shoot a western if you don't like
horses."
   -- Wim Wenders

ACKNOWLEDGMENTS

The illustration on the cover of this book was made by Grant Carmichael in 1990 when he was art editor of the Carnegie Mellon University student newspaper *The Tartan,* as a logo for my weekly column, entitled "JaviVision." That my Features editor, Allison Durazzi, kept the original art after all these years, and that Grant allowed us to use it on the cover, are both lovely acts of generosity. I loved that graphic back then, and I still do, though now more as a beautiful remembrance of hairlines (and eyeglass styles) gone by.

The Shamers are a creative turbine from which always emerges great power. I love you (in order of entrance into the group) Sarahs Kuhn and Watson, Margaret, Christina, Kate, Amber, Tom, Erik, Jay, Cecil, Liza, and Morgan.

The *Lost* fan community that developed at *The Fuselage* is responsible for my return to the online world after years of silence, and were the ground-zero audience for much of what eventually became these essays. They truly are a fandom like none other.

Io9.com, Apex Magazine and the *Los Angeles Review of Books* were all gracious enough to publish some of these pieces while letting me keep the right to collect them here. Charlie Jane Anders, Sigrid Ellis, and Sarah Mesle, respectively, edited my work for these publications, and my work is all the better for it.

For the record, Maureen Ryan has assured me that she will treat any future work of mine as harshly as possible in her work as a critic to compensate for her kind words.

Justin Horowitz and Liz Thurmond ought to get medals for their assistance in proofing the manuscript -- any mistakes you find are mine and not theirs. Jesse Freeman deserves a medal for her assistance in general.

Lee Thompson is Chief Designer of the Puppet Bureau, and don't you forget that.

My parents are a beacon of decency and insight. That the genetic lottery cursed them with me through no fault of their own is the most fortunate event of my life.

Finally, Sarah Baker Grillo should have a monument erected in her honor for taking on the burden of loving me. After battling the last few hundred pages, you probably want to give her a hug. I know I do.

ABOUT THE AUTHOR

Best known as one of the Emmy Award-winning producers of *Lost*, and creator of *The Middleman*, Javier Grillo-Marxuach is a prolific writer of films, comic books, essays and television. He also co-hosts the *Children of Tendu* podcast. Available free of charge on iTunes and at childrenoftendu.com, the podcast is designed to give newcomers guidance on how to navigate the entertainment industry with decency and integrity.